M. J. Trow studied history at university, after which he has spent years teaching. He is also an established crime writer and a biographer, with a reputation as a scholar who peels away legend to reveal the truth. Originally from Rhondda, South Wales, he lives in the Isle of Wight.

Highlights from the series

A Brief History of British Kings & Queens
Mike Ashley
A Brief History of the Crusades
Geoffrey Hindley
A Brief History of the Druids
Peter Berresford Ellis
A Brief History of the Dynasties of China
Bamber Gascoigne
A Brief Guide to the Greek Myths
Stephen Kershaw
A Brief History of Henry VIII
Derek Wilson
A Brief History of the Hundred Years War
Desmond Seward
A Brief History of Life in the Middle Ages
Martyn Whittock
A Brief History of Mankind
Cyril Aydon
A Brief History of the Middle East
Christopher Catherwood
A Brief History of the Private Lives of the Roman Emperors
Anthony Blond
A Brief History of Roman Britain
Joan P. Alcock
A Brief History of Secret Societies
David V. Barrett
A Brief History of Slavery
Jeremy Black
A Brief History of the Universe
J. P. McEvoy
A Brief History of Venice
Elizabeth Horodowich
A Brief History of the Vikings
Jonathan Clements

CLEOPATRA

ROBINSON

Constable & Robinson Ltd
55–56 Russell Square
London WC1B 4HP
www.constablerobinson.com

First published in the UK by Robinson,
an imprint of Constable & Robinson Ltd, 2013

A copy of the British Library Cataloguing in Publication
Data is available from the British Library

UK ISBN 978-184901-978-1

1 3 5 7 9 10 8 6 4 2

First published in the United States in 2011 by Running Press Book Publishers,
A Member of the Perseus Books Group

Books published by Running Press are available at special discounts for bulk purchases in the
United States by corporations, institutions, and other organizations.
For more information, please contact the Special Markets Department at the
Perseus Books Group, 2300 Chestnut Street, Suite 200, Philadelphia, PA 19103,
or call (800) 810-4145, ext. 5000, or e-mail special.markets@perseusbooks.com.

US ISBN 978-0-7624-4801-2
US Library of Congress Control Number: 2012942465

9 8 7 6 5 4 3 2 1
Digit on the right indicates the number of this printing

Running Press Book Publishers
2300 Chestnut Street
Philadelphia, PA 19103-4371

Visit us on the web!
www.runningpress.com

Printed and bound in the UK

MIX
Paper from
responsible sources
FSC® C018072

AUTHOR'S NOTE:

All dates are BC unless otherwise stated. I have also used modern spellings, which are now almost universal. So Kleopatra is Cleopatra, Marcus Antonius is Mark Antony, Gaius Pompeius is Pompey the Great, and so on. I have used Roman or Greek place names with their modern counterparts where necessary and have left currency as it was in the first century BC without any attempts to convert it into today's prices.

CONTENTS

BOOK ONE: ISIS BURNING

I

THE WORLD

ALEXANDRIA AD AEGYPTU, 27

Three years after the death of Queen Cleopatra, a Greek
traveller from Amisea in Pontus on the Black Sea arrived in
Egypt. His name was Strabo, the Squint-eyed, and he was
there on the staff of Greece's *praefectus* (governor), Gaius
Cornelius Gallus. It is likely that Strabo's boss was from
Frejus in southern Gaul (hence the name) and he was about
to be recalled to Rome to answer charges, possibly of
treason. Strabo could not fail to notice that there were a
large number of statues of Gallus dotted all over the place,
where there should have been nothing but statues of *his*
boss, Gaius Julius Caesar, known to us as Octavian. It was a
sign of the times that Octavian had begun, in the last months,
to call himself Augustus, the divinely ordained. It is no exaggeration to say that Augustus' status as first citizen (emperor

in all but name), and even his title, came about as a direct result of events in Egypt over the previous three years.

Strabo was a geographer, although, in the century before the birth of Christ, the science was rarely divorced from history and the whole package was an art, given to flights of fancy and downright fiction. Strabo wrote down what he saw in Egypt but he also believed all sorts of tittle-tattle fed to him by Romans, Alexandrians and Egyptians. The result, while short on accuracy, gives us a fascinating picture of the land that was Cleopatra's and which had just become Rome's newest province.

Inevitably, what impressed Strabo most was its capital, Alexandria. So astonishing was this and so different from the rest of the country that it was known as Alexandria ad Aegyptu – next to Egypt. If he had visited Rome recently, Strabo would have noticed the 'Egyptomania' sweeping that city – obelisks and archaic statuary were appearing in the Forum and at crossroads. Ironically, many Romans had worried that Cleopatra and her lover, the triumvir Marcus Antonius (Mark Antony) wanted to shift the capital of the empire to Alexandria. Now, it seemed, Alexandria was coming to Rome.

Cleopatra's Alexandria, the one Strabo marvelled at in 27, was 300 years old. Technically, Rome's population was larger, but the Italian city on its seven hills lacked the space, order and sumptuousness of the city founded by Alexander the Great. Like every other city in the ancient world, there was a mythical, supernatural story of its founding. More prosaically, the site was perfect. A small fishing village, Rakhotis, clustered on the shore between Lake Mareotis and the Mediterranean Sea. Alexander – and his general Ptolemy who began the actual building – needed links to Greece, his homeland of Macedonia and the rest of the empire he was carving out in the 320s; the sea provided that. The lake, via a series of canals, led to the Nile, the lifeblood of Egypt whose source, men said, was far to the south in the Mountains of the Moon. The city that Strabo saw was laid out on a lavish grid pattern, which divided the place into five districts – Alpha, Beta, Gamma, Delta and Epsilon – making Alexandria the first settlement in the world to have clear postal addresses. It was always a cosmopolitan city – Strabo could have talked Latin and Greek anywhere throughout it – but archaeological and other evidence implies that the ethnic groupings – Greek, Jew and Egyptian – kept to themselves in their quarters. Inevitably, in a city founded by the Greeks, it was they who were Alexandria's elite, scholars and merchants living in grand limestone and marble houses nearest to the vast sprawl of the royal palaces in the Beta district. Only they, at first, could become full citizens.

Strabo had been told – and there is no reason to doubt this – that the Ptolemies who had ruled Egypt for three centuries had been inveterate builders, each one adding another palace extension to commemorate their reign. By 27 these buildings, where both Cleopatra and Antony had died by their own hands, covered between a quarter and a third of the city. On the island of Pharos, the first Ptolemy commissioned one of the seven wonders of the world – a 328-foot-tall lighthouse made of gleaming white stone. It was the tallest building the Greeks ever erected, and Rome never surpassed it. On top was a huge statue of Zeus Soter (the saviour father of the gods) and a series of mirrors that reflected a perpetual flame that shone into the night. Strabo says the lighthouse had many tiers (contemporary depictions show three) and that each stage had a different shape – rectangular, octagonal and cylindrical – probably to show off Greek architectural skill or to give the colossal edifice strength.[1]

From the lighthouse, a causeway called the Heptastadion[2] ran to the city, dividing the harbour into two. Kitosis (the Box) was the city's dockyard where Cleopatra's war-galleys and river barges would have been built. The eastern harbour was Megas Limen (which the Romans called Portus Magnus) and the western, rather smaller, was Eunostos (the Happy Return). It was into these sheltered waters that Cleopatra sailed her warship the *Antonia* in September 31, the decks bright with flowers and garlands, as though returning from a victory. In fact, she had just left the more turbulent and bloody waters of Actium, which marked the beginning of her end.

Strabo, the Greek scholar, would have been most fascinated by the Museion, the place of the cure of the soul, which was the largest library in the world. Ptolemy I and his successors borrowed works of Greek culture over the years from Delphi and elsewhere and copied them – they sent the copies back and kept the originals themselves. These books (actually scrolls) and the scholars who floated around them, copying and researching, were at the disposal of the child Cleopatra in her time, and of her children by Julius Caesar and Mark Antony. Never again would so much scholarship be concentrated in one place, although a section of the building and its contents had been destroyed twenty years before when Caesar used the adjacent Great Theatre as his headquarters against the army of Cleopatra's brother, Ptolemy XIII.

Strabo would have seen the Soma, the dazzling tomb of Alexander with its Egyptian-style gold sarcophagus in a translucent glass case. People came from all over the world to pay homage to the greatest general in history and Strabo would have heard the story of three years earlier, when Octavian had come calling to claim the country as his own. He had demanded the removal of the sarcophagus lid and had strewn the embalmed hero with flowers. In doing so, he accidentally knocked off Alexander's nose. Strabo may have seen, but does not mention, the tombs of Antony and Cleopatra, lying side by side in death as they did in life. He may have known that Octavian had refused to visit the tombs of the earlier Ptolemies and probably thought it best not to mention his own visit, if he made one. The newly half-deified Augustus did not tolerate opposition, as Gallus was about to find out.

Strabo saw the huge temple of Poseidon, the sea-god; the Great Caesarium, still under construction, as Cleopatra's own memorial to Julius Caesar. In AD 40, Alexandria's home-grown Jewish philosopher Philo wrote of this place:

> For there is elsewhere no precinct like that which is called the Sebastium, a temple to Caesar on the shipboard, situated on an eminence facing the harbours ... huge and conspicuous, fitted on a scale not found elsewhere with dedicated offerings, around it a girdle of pictures and statues in silver and gold, forming a precinct of vast breadth, embellished with porticoes, libraries, chambers, groves, gateways and wide open courts and everything which lavish expenditure could produce to beautify it.[3]

He would have walked through the marble colonnades to the Temple of Saturn and the Gymnasion, which served as a public forum for the rulers of Alexandria and had been the site of ghastly wholesale slaughters by Cleopatra's ancestors. He would also have seen the Timonium, a sad little summer house near the harbour that Mark Antony had built on his return from Actium, unable for a while to function or to face the world. Most famous of all, Strabo would have visited the Serapion, a temple designed to unite the Greek and Egyptian gods in a successful working partnership that lasted for 300 years.

It may be that Strabo noted the vast difference between the hush and academic peace of the royal palaces, now empty of the Ptolemies and only partly occupied by Gallus[4] and the bustle of the cosmopolitan city outside its walls. Here, in the quarters, lived and worked the multi-nationals whose ancestors had sometimes toppled kings and pharaohs. The trading vessels groaned with wheat, linen, glass, perfumes, spices and papyri from the Nile and Africa to the south. The city itself was famed for its glass, pottery, baskets and linen. All human life was there, the descendants of men and women who had known rule by Egyptians, Persians, Greeks and now Romans.

Somewhere in the city, Strabo saw the cemeteries that housed Alexandria's dead, probably laid out to the east and west of the palaces. Here was the Nemesion, the temple of retribution built by Julius Caesar to house the severed head of his rival Gaius Pompeius (Pompey the Great) who had been murdered on the shore not far away.

The geographer was clearly impressed by the splendour of Cleopatra's city but the Roman puritan in him was never far below the surface. Wandering around the Navalia, the dockyards, he noted 'on boats [there was] flute-playing and dancing without restraint, with the utmost lewdness'.[5] Cleopatra's father had been called Auletes, the flute-player, by the Greeks, and was also called Neo Dionysus, a reincarnation of the drunken god whom the upright Romans despised as Bacchus. It was a reminder, if one was needed, that Egypt's way was not Rome's way and that Gallus and his successors had a duty to do something about this.

Sailing up the Nile, Strabo was transported back in time. The story of Cleopatra was essentially the story of Alexandria and of Rome. Alone of her family, she had learned the Egyptian demotic language and sailed the river often to worship at the various cult shrines along the way, but for most of her life she lived in an alien Greek city and died there, brought to suicide by Roman politics. There is a sense in which, whoever ruled from Alexandria, life for the people along the Nile remained the same. The country was long and narrow, skirting the river that was its lifeblood. Some areas were so remote the Romans never reached them and the Egyptians were a simple, superstitious and inbred people where incest was perfectly common in the natural order of things. Someone told Herodotus of Halicarnassus in the fifth century that women here urinated standing up and the men sitting down. In a society in which people worshipped crocodiles and bowed to gods with the heads of jackals, hawks and baboons, why should he doubt it? At Babylon Fossatum, Strabo came upon a huge army camp, one of those rectangular bastions of empire, built solidly of earthworks, ramparts, towers and palisades. Three legions were based here, the men who had fought first for Antony, then for Octavian in the miserable, dishonourable war that had just finished. One hundred and fifty slaves toiled under the murderous Egyptian sun on a giant treadmill that lifted drinking water for the 2,000 men in the camp. Strabo would have noticed that the fresh sea breezes of Alexandria were far away and the towns and villages along the river small, cramped and dirty.

It was the history of the place, as much as the geography, that captivated him. He saw the pyramids, already ancient when Rome was a cluster of huts; and sphinxes, those strange, crouching animalistic gods half-buried in the ever shifting sand. He visited the sacred bull of Apis, which Octavian had refused to see and which Cleopatra had worshipped, as had all her predecessors. At Arsinoe, he came across Crocodilopolis, a shrine where the priests lovingly looked after a sacred crocodile. 'It is called Petesuchos,' Strabo recorded,[6] 'and is fed on grain and bits of meat and wine, which are always offered to it by the visiting foreigners.'[7] The animal also wore gold 'earrings' and bracelets on his forefeet.

What Strabo was looking at was a country in decline. The Ptolemies had ruled this land for 300 years and had amassed a fortune in doing so. Egypt was rich and the principal supplier of grain for Rome and its empire, but the general sense that Strabo had was similar to that of the English poet Shelley eighteen centuries later. Egypt was an 'antique land' in desperate need of renovation. In Strabo's day, the Romans had only been there for three years and it was clearly early days. Even so, he wrote that 'to the best of their abilities they have, I might say, set most things right'.[8]

The floor mosaic in a sanctuary at Praenoste near Rome, dating from around Cleopatra's time, shows the Nile in full flood as the Romans imagined it. Exotic animals – lions, giraffes, rhinoceros, hippopotami, giant centipedes, camels and others clearly invented in the artist's imagination – are caught by the rising waters, and towers and temples stand like islands in the torrent. It is not accurate (unsurprisingly) and although an astonishing work of art, does not help us understand Cleopatra's country very well. One of the queen's recent biographers, Stacy Schiff, astutely observes that Cleopatra is absent when there is no Roman in the room. This has nothing to do with the queen herself and everything to do with the Egyptian and Roman methods of recording history. Rome, in the form of its language and its law, continued to dominate intellectual Europe for the next 1,500 years. Scholars of later generations venerated Rome as one of the great civilizations of the ancient world, so *anything* a Roman had to say, about kingship, war, religion, even how to handle slaves and what sort of hat to wear in the sun, became hugely important and was preserved. Egypt, by contrast, was a culture of a very different sort and not 'discovered' until Napoleon's invasion of the country in 1798. Egyptian records were curiously parochial, as if there was no world outside the land along the Nile and the bas-reliefs and the tomb paintings reflect a world of men interacting with gods in a half-understood magic. There are no Egyptian gossips, at least none whose writings have survived.

One particular blank – which could not be filled in by Strabo and is difficult to fill at all – is the daily routines of Egypt in Cleopatra's time. There is a timeless quality about ancient history. When we look at the giant bas-reliefs on temples at Karnak, Dendera and Luxor, we are looking at gods from 3,000 years earlier still being worshipped in Cleopatra's reign. The men rowing on the Nile are doing so in boats that have not changed for two millennia. They are cutting down reeds and wheat at harvest time exactly as their forebears had done for centuries. No one comments on this because it had been a way of life for so long that it was not worthy of comment. Strabo waxes lyrical about Alexandria's library because it was unique. He tells us almost nothing about the fishermen at the waterside because there were so many of them. The way of life was agricultural and the success of the harvest – geared entirely to the Nile's movements – made the difference between life and death. Since almost all our records of Cleopatra come from the pens of her enemies and just occasionally from her own priests, it is almost impossible to see the real woman. To the Romans, she was *fatale monstrum*, an unnatural creature to be destroyed. To the priests of Memphis, the ancient Egyptian capital, she was the embodiment of the goddess Aphrodite whom they called Isis. We are forever doomed to see her through a distorted glass.

Nevertheless, for all the colour, excitement and ultimate tragedy of her life, she ruled Egypt for nineteen years, so we must agree that she was actually extraordinarily good at her job. How did her government work? Egypt's population is impossible to determine. Diodorus Siculus, who visited the country when the future queen was ten years old, estimated it at about three million, but this was probably (and unusually for a Roman) a conservative estimate. Most experts today light on seven million – about the population of Greater London. The country was divided into two geographically – Lower Egypt meant the delta, dominated of course by the artificially created 'alien' city of Alexandria, and Upper Egypt, which followed the tortuous mean-derings of the Nile into the swamplands of the Sudan. Occasionally there had been rebellions from the south against earlier Ptolemies but in more recent times most of the trouble for the ruling family came from Alexandria itself. Even here, the various ethnic groups tended to operate side by side rather than in unity. The native Egyptians had their own culture, language, priests and law; so did the Jews, who wrote and spoke Aramaic; and of course the Greeks who saw themselves as culturally superior to anybody.

At the apex of Egyptian society were the Ptolemies themselves, personified between 48 and 30 by Cleopatra. They had ruled with varying degrees of success for 300 years, but as pharaohs (the word means literally 'great house') they tapped into a system that was 1,000 years old. The role of pharaoh was what it remained in all civilized countries for centuries – he (or in the case of Egypt, sometimes, she) was head of government, commander-in-chief of army and navy, law-giver and, crucially, a semi-divine link between man and the gods. We shall examine the crucial role of religion, superstition and myth in the next chapter, but we must bear it in mind throughout this book. Egyptian, Greek and Roman culture did not exist without this 'other world', which paralleled the more humdrum existence on earth.

Below the Ptolemies came an upper-class[9] elite – aristocrats, bureaucrats and priests who oiled the wheels of government. These posts were usually hereditary, so that when Pasherentptah, Cleopatra's high priest, died, it was natural that his son Petubastis should take over, even though the boy was only seven years old. The priests were administrators, lawyers and doctors. Their temples were not only shrines but places of refuge and an important role of the priesthood was to monitor the levels of the Nile, the Egyptian equivalent of watching the stock exchange today in terms of national economy. The Roman republican system, of officials elected for a year and being unable to stand again for ten, would have made no sense at all to the Ptolemies or their people. It is unfortunate for us that the men of their class did not, unlike their Roman counterparts, write letters or gossip about each other, so we do not have the same sense of day-to-day realism from the Ptolemaic court. That many of them were highly unscrupulous, however, cannot be doubted from the events of Cleopatra's reign. Her brother's tutor and her army commander plotted her overthrow and murder in 49. When we have examples of Cleopatra intervening personally, it is almost always to deal with a greedy or over-zealous tax collector.

Unusual in the court were the eunuchs, people the Romans found repellent. These men were respected in Alexandria and trusted largely because sex was not likely to feature in any political machinations and high-born families' girls were safe from molestation. Since Roman law forbade castration, even for slaves (which the eunuchs usually were), men like Octavian saw them as yet another tragic example of the way in which Egypt's women emasculated men.

Under the elite were what we might loosely term the middle class. As usual in pre-industrial societies, this ambitious, articulate and educated group were probably relatively few in number. Included in this category were the merchants and craftsmen who made and sold the goods that made Egypt (and the Ptolemies through taxation) rich. At the bottom were the masses – peasants who lived in mud-brick hovels along the Nile and in the delta and worked as farm labourers and fishermen. These were the men who dragged the huge blocks of stone for the pyramids and sphinxes that Strabo marvelled at. Life was not completely static for them. The Ptolemies introduced new farming policies, irrigated fields, dammed the Nile and diverted the river in places. Iron blades replaced bronze for the sickles and scythes used at harvest time, but essentially, these people were the timeless ones, anonymous in their lives, unmarked in their deaths. Their generic type is shown in carving and in paint on scores of walls of tombs and temples in ancient Egyptian kingdoms. The Nile flooded in late summer and the new crop was grown in autumn. After the spring harvest, the dry season came with a burning wind from the west. And the whole cycle began again. Even today, standing below the great pyramid at Giza, it is almost unreal to see the Nile, a bright strip of living green at the edge of the limitless sand.

In the fifth century, Herodotus visited the country. It was the Greeks who called the incomprehensible river Neilos; before that the Egyptians knew it as *pa iteru aa*, the great river. Sometimes, according to legend , it flowed with gold. Ancient Egyptian tombs were called pyramids after Greek cakes of the same shape. Tall, tapering monoliths became obelisks (kebab skewers). Long before the Ptolemies replaced the Persians as Egypt's rulers, the Greeks were rewriting the country's culture. Apart from the peculiar urination habits of men and women, Herodotus commented on the almost complete reversal of customs in Egypt. Women bartered in the market-places while men stayed at home and did the weaving. Even here, the looms operated the other way from the Greeks'. Men carried loads on their heads; women on their shoulders. Men did not have to support their parents in their old age; women did. Men had two sets of clothes; women only one. Women carried their babies for fewer weeks than anywhere else – twins and triplets were common. Goats gave birth to five kids rather than the usual two. Pigeons laid twelve eggs, not the commonplace ten. The Nile had living in its mudbanks creatures that were half mice, half sand. The river's odd behaviour, the people's odd behaviour, all seemed strange to a civilized visitor, but the Greek Herodotus was every bit as much a 'johnny-come-lately' as Strabo was four hundred years later and the Ptolemies had learned to cope with the strangeness of the place.

By Cleopatra's time, a top-heavy civil service had been streamlined and in the rare glimpses we have of the queen at work running her country, she often intervenes personally, particularly against corrupt officials. The country was divided into forty *nomoi* (local districts), which all had Greek names by the first century BC. The local governor was the *strategos* (general) who worked for Cleopatra under the over-arching *epistrategos*, who we can regard as a sort of chief minister. The elite at court were inevitably Greek – even the Ptolemies' bodyguards were Macedonians – and this sometimes caused trouble. If an Egyptian wanted to get on, he would have to learn Greek and hope for an appointment. Apart from Cleopatra herself, few Greeks bothered to learn Egyptian.

The government kept a tight control on the economy, which is one reason why Cleopatra was the richest woman in the world at the time. Everybody in Egypt paid taxes, whether it was on salt, fields, drainage ditches or baths. The government also controlled a rudimentary banking system, which issued gold and silver coinage (which frequently had to be debased for economic reasons) and had a monopoly of the textiles, oil and papyrus industries. Cleopatra had several textile workshops of her own, operated by slave women.

Since virtually all the land belonged to Cleopatra, she kept a careful watch, via her bureaucratic record-keepers, on how it was used. Change of usage, perhaps from wheat field to olive grove, needed royal permission. No one could leave their *nome* (or province) and an army of officials checked inventories, looms and breweries with a thoroughness that makes the Norman Domesday Book in England 1,000 years later look positively amateur.

In one important aspect, the Egypt of the Ptolemies paved the way for the legend of Cleopatra. Greek women – and even more so Roman women – lived in a legal and moral straitjacket designed by men. The Egyptians were more free and easy. So from the century before Cleopatra we find Graeco-Egyptian marriages taking place, in which both languages were spoken in the home and children got used to different names. Women owned property, ran businesses and walked alone in the streets. Those privately taught at home (there were still no formal schools for them) could become doctors, artists, musicians and lawyers. They were rare, but they were there. When the Romans discovered one of them, Cleopatra VII, behaving in this way, they were outraged. Two who were not were Julius Caesar and Mark Antony and, indirectly, they both paid for it with their lives.

2

THE OTHER WORLD

EGYPT, 332

The story of Cleopatra is so well known to us via Shakespeare and the silver screen that we tend to believe we understand her. Her storms and her calms make sense because we are just the same as her. Only 2,000 years separate us and people are people no matter when they live. Whether we see Cleopatra as a seductress, a whore or as a consummate politician and a loving wife and mother, we do so because the events of her life allow us to make comparisons with our own emotions and experiences. Most of us have never been queen of Egypt, nor have we slept with Roman dictators, but we can empathize with the decisions she made, born of the experiences she faced.

Where we cannot see her, for the choking fog of incense, is in the religious dimension of her life. And not only hers, but everyone's in her story. 'It is almost impossible,' writes Guy de la Bédoyère, one of the best 'Roman' experts today, 'to measure the quality and nature of symbolism, ritual and belief. One man's religious symbol is another man's decorative motif and yet another's nightmare.'[10]

So, three years before Strabo reached Egypt, Octavian caused grave offence to the hereditary priests of the country by refusing to have anything to do with the Apis bull, so revered by them and by Cleopatra. 'I worship gods, not animals,' he sneered. In 332, when Alexander of Macedon came to Egypt on his way to the creation of his vast and impossible to maintain empire, he had a dream. His hero Homer came to him and told him to found a great city at that spot on the coast where King Menelaus of Sparta had found himself stranded on his way home from the war with Troy. Our cynical, modern, western world has no time for any of this. Of course, Octavian was right to rubbish a bull and we find his pantheon of gods led by Jupiter to be equally nonsensical. The Trojan War as Homer told it never happened, so how could he know where or even if Menelaus came to Egypt? And even if it were true, what sort of reason is that to found a city? To make these points is to miss the point. These things were real to the Egyptians, the Greeks, the Romans, every bit as much as God, Allah, Amida Nyorai and Vahig⁻ur⁻u are real to some people today. Unless we understand that dreams, omens, prophecies and ritual were an essential part of the lives of the Ptolemies, the Caesars, the Antonys, we shall not see the real Cleopatra at all.

When Alexander of Macedon marched at the head of his invading army into Egypt 300 years before Cleopatra was born, he came to Per-Baster, the shrine of the cat-goddess

Bastet. This was the capital of the eighteenth *nome* of Lower Egypt and Greek travellers before Alexander equated the goddess with their own Artemis, the huntress. This divine equation happened everywhere. Later invaders would dismiss other gods as superstition and mumbo-jumbo but the Greeks (and, to a lesser extent, the Romans) assumed they were the familiar deities but known by different names. The goddess was portrayed by Alexander's time as a cat-headed woman, carrying a sacred sistrum rattle and a basket. She was the goddess of dancing and music, able to fend off disease and evil spirits. Herodotus wrote of great pilgrimages to Per-Baster (which the Greeks called Bubastis), which brought thousands down the Nile in barges to the melody of flutes and the rhythm of the sistrums. Alexander's men would have been astonished by the number of mummified cats buried in and around the city.

The army's next port of call was Iunu, the city of the sun that the Greeks called Heliopolis. This was the cult centre of the sun-god Ra, who was born each morning, was a man by midday and died every evening in old age. This god was so all-powerful – he equates with the Greek Zeus and the Roman Jupiter – that he could assume any shape and went by a number of aliases. From him sprang many of the gods of ancient Egypt – Isis and Osiris, Shu and Tefut, Geb and Nut, Set and Nephthys, all of whom were worshipped at Heliopolis as 'the divine company'.

Everywhere that Alexander went he was within sight of giant stone representations of the Egyptian gods and the men who, as pharaohs, had lived as living gods, waiting to join the rest in the afterlife. Alexander was welcomed as a liberator in the towns and cities he marched through because he was clearing out the hated Persians and he understood very well that the force with which he had to reckon were the priests. When all was said and done, the pharaoh was only one man, albeit divine. The priesthood was everywhere, the guardians of history, the literate keepers of records, the go-betweens between the pharaoh-god and his people and recognizable instantly by their shaved heads. Plato said, 'In Egypt, it is not possible for a king to rule without the help of the priests.'[11] At Memphis, the ancient Egyptian capital, Alexander was welcomed by the high priest Maatranefer, the 'master-builder'.

Memphis was in many ways the most holy city of Egypt. Ptah was worshipped here, the creator-god particularly associated with artisans and artists. His effigies usually showed an embalmed figure, wrapped in a winding sheet and head tightly bandaged under the elaborate mummification process. Only his hands are free and in them he holds a sceptre symbolizing omnipotence and stability. Again, he had a number of aliases and was known to ward off dangerous animals and the inevitable evil spirits. The name Egypt derives from Ptah, so the god was very senior in the pantheon of deities. Herodotus, visiting Memphis 200 years before Alexander, was shown the sites of Ptah's miracles and the nearby temple of Imhotep, the first shrine the Macedonians would have seen that commemorated a man, rather than a god. Imhotep had been the chief architect of King Zoser in the third dynasty and had built Egypt's first pyramid. The Greeks translated his name as Imuthes, he who comes in peace, and he was associated with learning and culture of all sorts, but especially of medicine. In that respect, the later Greeks equated him with Asclepius, and by Cleopatra's reign, Imhotep seems to have replaced Ptah as the central god at Memphis.

It was at Memphis that Alexander came across the bull cult that continued to dominate Egyptian religion until Cleopatra's time. The bull, of course, as a symbol of strength and fertility, was common to Greek spirituality, too. Alexander's own horse was called Bucephalus, the bull-headed. In Memphis, the Apis bull was venerated. This animal was sacred to Ptah and his reincarnation. This was no ordinary beast, and the priests who tended it lovingly were looking for a very specific hide colouring. Ptah had insemi-nated a virgin heifer in his guise of heavenly fire and the resulting offspring had to have a white triangle on its forehead, a vulture-shape along its back, a crescent moon on its left flank, a scarab (beetle) shape on its tongue and a double tail. Our cynical age can only assume that a lot of painting and/or wishful thinking went on for priests to continue to find an exact replacement for the bull when the old one died. The Apis bull could tell the future and was consulted much as the Greeks checked regularly with their Oracle at Delphi. The Persians, during their occupancy of Egypt, had twice assassinated the bull and the whole nation had been distraught at the news. At Sakkara, which Alexander also visited, the mummified corpses of these sacred bulls were found by archaeologists in AD 1850. The temple there was called the Serapeum because the dead bull was equated with Osiris, god of the underworld. The far better known Serapeum (Osiris-Apis), which Cleopatra would have known, was built in Alexandria later. The god Serapis, several carvings of whom have been found recently in underwater archaeological digs in the old harbour, was a perfect example of the halfway house between Egyptian and Greek theology. It would be wrong to think of the Serapia as silent, grim mausoleums. They were places of regular pilgrimage, with music, noise and a thriving tourist trade in 'bull memorabilia'. Professional female mourners were employed to wail and beat their breasts in grief.

When Alexander was crowned pharaoh of Egypt on 14 November 332 he was described during the ceremony as 'Horus, the strong ruler who takes the lands of the foreigners' and 'beloved of Amun and the chosen one of Ra'. In one sense, these gods were interchangeable, but whereas Ra was linked with the sun, Amun was associated with fertility and reproduction. In effigy, he was shown sometimes as a pharaoh with a crown on his head and a flail in his hand. Elsewhere he is carved as a ram with curling horns. It is intriguing that in various coins he had minted, Alexander is shown with ram's horns in his hair or as part of his helmet. It is possible that, by a circuitous route over the centuries, the idea of the horned god and the devil came from this tradition. Often referred to as 'his mother's husband', Amun represented the pharaonic tradition, continued by the Ptolemies, of incestuous relationships to keep the bloodline pure. Amun-Ra lit the day and even lent a glow to the night, since his light could never be completely extinguished. He also won victories over his enemies, so it was the perfect honorary title to give to Alexander.

As pharaoh, Alexander, like Cleopatra 300 years later, was Egypt's highest priest and the role was vitally important. In January 331, he travelled west from the Nile delta into Cyrenia (today's Libya) and got lost in a Saharan sandstorm. Two black ravens appeared and led the expedition to safety. Giving thanks at a temple of Amun, Alexander followed the shrine's priest into subterranean passageways and emerged later firm in the belief that he was indeed the son of a god. The transition then from ancient Egypt with its animal deities to the Ptolemies with their Greek overlay of religion was assured from the start. It would continue right through to the reign of Cleopatra, after which the Romans dismissed the whole thing as superstition. It is difficult to say when beliefs of this sort disappeared. The arrival of Islam in the seventh century AD certainly drove them underground and eventually eclipsed them, but there is some evidence to believe that Alexander as a living god was still being worshipped 1,000 years after that.

The Ptolemies continued the linked Graeco-Egyptian cult tradition. Arsinoe II, whose sole rule was in some ways a blueprint for Cleopatra's, was born as 'Daughter of Ra' and 'Daughter of Geb' (the father of Isis). The pharaonic regalia worn by all the Ptolemies, including Cleopatra, reflect those centuries-old traditions. The red crown was Geb's. The ram's horns were Amun's; the double plumes, cow horns and sun disc belonged to Hathor-Isis. Hathor was Ra's daughter, the golden one, known to the Greeks as Aphrodite. She is the great heavenly cow, but always shown with a human body and face. The sistrum, a rattle to frighten away evil, is always associated with her, and her shrine at Dendera along the Nile was built to resemble a series of giant rattles. She protected women especially and became linked with motherhood, beauty and love. She was the 'lady of the sycamore', hiding in those trees on the edge of the desert and welcoming the dead, who had just climbed her long ladder to heaven, with bread and water. At Dendera, her 'day' marked the beginning of the new year and was an excuse for parties, dancing, music and a great deal of drink!

It is with Isis that we most closely associate Cleopatra. The Greeks knew the goddess by a variety of names because she was so all-powerful. She is Selene, the moon; Demeter the corn-goddess; Aphrodite, the goddess of love and sex. In Egyptian belief, Isis was the wife of Osiris, god of the underworld, and their son was Horus, the musician, usually shown as a falcon. The fullest description we have of her story comes from Plutarch, the Romanized Greek who has left us most details on Cleopatra, too. Out of that emerges the notion of embalming, which a distraught Isis carried out on her murdered husband whose body had been dismembered by his brother Set. So clever was Isis that she became indispensible to Ra, enabling him to recover from a deadly snake bite and her future was assured.

She was still being worshipped along the Nile long after Christianity arrived in the fourth century AD and so important was her cult that shrines to her appear all over the Graeco-Roman world as far north as the Rhine in what is today Germany. Her festivals were held in spring and autumn and she is so all-embracing that she is linked with birth and with death and almost everything in between. She is the goddess of sailing and even the 'wet nurse of the crocodile'.

Not for nothing did Cleopatra work very hard to make herself regarded as the living Isis.

BOOK TWO:
DAUGHTER OF THE GENERAL

3

THE SUCCESSOR AND THE SAVIOUR

NEBUCHADNEZZAR'S PALACE, BABYLON, 323

On the first day, he drank and partied with Medius before bathing, sleeping and partying again far into the night. He ate a little, then went to sleep. The fever was already on him.

On the second day he was carried on a litter to perform out the usual sacrifices and he rested in the men's apartments until dusk. He gave his officers orders about the coming expedition: the army would march on the fourth day; he would go by ship a day later. They carried him to his boat and he sailed across to a garden where he bathed and rested...

...On the eighth day, though very weak, he managed to make the sacrifices. He asked the generals to stay in the hall with the brigadiers and colonels in front of the doors. He was carried back from the garden to the Royal Apartments. He recognized the officers as they passed before him, but said nothing.

And on the tenth day, he died. He was Alexander of Macedon, known as 'the Great' and perhaps the greatest general in history. He was thirty-two. In eleven years he had destroyed the mighty Persian Empire and his territory extended from the Danube in the north-west to the Indus in the east. Such military brilliance would never be seen again,[12] but the problem with power based on one man is that when that man is gone, a vast hole is left behind. In an age when rulers passed on their power to members of their families, Alexander's son was still unborn and his brother, Philip Arrhidaios, was a halfwit.

In the last days of his life, Alexander urged his generals to divide the empire among themselves. The problem was that he was dying from what was probably cerebral malaria; his speech was rambling and his intentions unclear. Did he expect one man to succeed him? Or was he orchestrating a bloodbath on Darwinian lines of survival of the fittest? One modern historian refers to the decision as Alexander's funeral games. The generals who had been prepared to follow Alexander to the ends of the earth would not do that for each other and conflict was inevitable.

The symbolic farewells that Alexander made on 9 June 323 only added to the divisiveness. Perdiccas, his highest-ranking lieutenant, was given his signet ring but it was to Ptolemy that Alexander gave his personal possessions and it was Ptolemy who mounted a vigil in the temple of Serapis, the Graeco-Egyptian god whose carved image Alexander carried with him on campaign. Fighting broke out almost immediately, literally around Alexander's corpse before the embalmers had gone to work. On the one side were officers under Perdiccas who wanted to govern the empire in the name of Alexander's unborn son; on the other were those who backed the adult but highly biddable Arrhidaios. It was a no-win situation in terms of stability, but at the birth of Alexander IV in the autumn, he and his uncle were declared joint rulers.

The real power, of course, was the army, a huge fighting force then unrivalled in the world. Perdiccas was in overall control but under him Antigonas ruled Asia Minor, Lysimachos held Thrace (modern Bulgaria), Seleucus had Babylonia, Antipatros claimed Macedonia and the Greek city states. Ptolemy was, according to the Roman chronicler Arrian, 'appointed to govern Egypt and Libya and those lands of the Arabs that were contiguous to Egypt; and Cleomenes who had been made governor by Alexander was subordinated to Ptolemy'.[13]

If this was Ptolemy's idea, it was a shrewd move; if it wasn't, he made the most of it. Egypt was the most southerly of Alexander's territories. On the map it looks like a geographical afterthought almost separated from the rest by a narrow land strip at Gaza. Given the speed of communications in the ancient world, Ptolemy might have known he could hold this land for ever, even without his former leader's affection for it.

As we have seen, Alexander had marched unopposed into Egypt in October 332 and, backed by the fleet sailing south from the Nile delta and along the river itself, he came to Memphis, the ancient Egyptian capital, in triumph.

For years, Egypt had lain under the yoke of Persian domination. In fact, some of the towns Alexander marched through were rubble as a result. Unlike the Persians, the Greeks acknowledged, respected and honoured the lands they conquered. True, they equated the Egyptian pantheon of gods with their own and the Greek culture that they imposed never assimilated with the native one, but

Alexander and all his Egyptian successors for 300 years understood the importance of working with the priesthood and nobility, not against them. It was a master-class in empire-building.

The Egyptians, recognizing divinity in Alexander or perhaps realizing he could not be defeated, declared him the successor of Nectanebo, the last native king of Egypt. He was now pharaoh of Upper and Lower Egypt, 'beloved of Amun and the chosen one of Ra', and on his deathbed the conqueror whispered that he wanted his body to lie with Amun, hedging his bets perhaps on the existence of an afterlife.

He planned a great city on the Mediterranean coast south of the tiny island of Pharos and in this respect, Alexandrine Egypt would be very different from the ancient country along the Nile, based on Memphis, Thebes and Luxor. Here, at the city named after him, would be built the biggest library in the world and it would be a home to the finest scholars. It would grow and flourish as Alexandria ad Aegyptu to the Romans – Alexandria next to Egypt – an apt metaphor for the cultures that never quite meshed.

So Ptolemy's choice of Egypt was a good one and, as if to underline the fact and his own closeness to Alexander, he took his master's embalmed body, in its glittering Egyptian-style sarcophagus, back to the Nile. Perdiccas saw this as an act of treachery. He was anxious to preserve his own position as Alexander's successor and needed to have the body to prove it.[14] Claiming that the body should be interred in Macedonian soil, at Aegae, Perdiccas pursued Ptolemy with a huge force. At Damascus, Ptolemy cleverly switched corpses and continued into Egypt with the real body, leaving Perdiccas to find that the great hearse hung with battle trophies was empty.

This marked the first of many wars among the successors of Alexander, which may, of course, have been what he intended, but Perdiccas' invasion of Egypt in 321 was a disaster. He lost 2,000 men crossing the Nile at Memphis, their blood mingling with the water as the crocodiles had a field day and Perdiccas himself, facing a mutiny, was murdered.

With peace at home in Egypt and no immediate rivals on the horizon, Ptolemy began a settled regime. He didn't take the title of king until 305 and like the other successors to Alexander, could claim that he was still acting as regent on behalf of the infant Alexander IV. He had the conqueror's body buried with Graeco-Egyptian solemnity in Nectanebo's tomb in the Serapeum at Memphis until the final resting place could be made ready in Alexandria.

The murder and mayhem that we associate with Cleopatra's family (see Chapter 4) could be found anywhere in the ancient world and by 305, all of Alexander's immediate family were dead. Ptolemy was sixty by now and known as 'Soter', the saviour, a title given to him by the inhabitants of the island of Rhodes to whose rescue he came during his reign. His coins show a strong profile with a prominent hooked nose, which was a characteristic of later Ptolemies and may explain his adoption of the eagle as his personal badge. In the ancient world such symbols were hugely important. In Cleopatra's day, the eagle had been adopted by Rome (perhaps because of links with Egypt) and Gaius Pompeius (Pompey the Great) deliberately styled his dashing cavalry tactics on those of Alexander, even copying the conqueror's hairstyle!

We shall look at the heirs of Ptolemy in the next chapter – and it is little short of astonishing that the family should hold on to power in Egypt for three centuries before

Cleopatra bit off more than she could chew against the might of increasingly imperial Rome. Cleopatra was, according to some historians, thirty-two parts Greek, twenty-seven parts Macedonian and five parts Persian. The fact that bas-reliefs from her time and various descriptions of her in 'fact' and fiction ever since often portray her as purely Egyptian misses the vital starting point of her line. It began with a rough-and-ready soldier, a capable general and steadfast friend, who, against all the odds, died in his bed at the age of eighty-four.

Ptolemy I, the successor and saviour, was cremated according to Macedonian custom and his ashes were placed alongside Alexander's embalmed body in the city they both had built.

4

THE FAMILY FROM HELL

ALEXANDRIA, 287

Cleopatra's family tree has been described as more like a cobweb, tangled and, in its own way, deadly. Looking back as we are from 2,000 years later, two things emerge. First is the sheer confusion in a bloodline that contains Ptolemies, Arsinoes and Cleopatras by the dozen. 'Our' Cleopatra is the seventh of that name – and the last.[15] It is practical to use Roman numerals for them – Ptolemy I, Ptolemy II and so on – and the ever-cynical Alexandrians usually gave them unflattering nicknames. So Ptolemy I Soter (saviour) got off very lightly, but Ptolemy VIII was Physcon (the Fat-bellied) and his father, Ptolemy VII was Neos Philopator (the New Father-loving). The other problem is much more difficult for us to grasp. Elimination by murder was the stock-in-trade of many ruling families in this period, but it was particularly prevalent among the Ptolemies. On the one hand, intermarriage between brothers and sisters, uncles and nieces – which was a Macedonian as well as an Egyptian custom – kept the bloodline pure and perhaps ought to have made for greater harmony. On the other, power politics was clearly more important than bloodlines or emotions, and assassinations were orchestrated on a regular basis. This extended to Cleopatra herself and is another way in which her 'infinite variety' is difficult for a twenty-first-century readership to comprehend.

Ptolemy Soter made his younger son Ptolemy co-regent in 287, marking a sort of semi-retirement. The younger Ptolemy was married to a daughter of another of Alexander's successors, Lysimachos of Thrace, which might have created a unifying situation and helped bind Alexander's empire. The fly in the ointment, however, was Ptolemy II's sister, Arsinoe II, who had been married to Lysimachos herself. In an extraordinarily tangled example of family realpolitik, Arsinoe attempted to dispose of her own rivals and those of her children by turning to yet another successor, Seleucus of Babylonia, for help. By 275 she had married her brother Ptolemy II and become co-regent.

It was this Macedonian–Egyptian system of giving supreme political power to women that the Romans could not handle in Cleopatra's day. Roman women were supposed to be virtuous, supportive of their husbands and excellent mothers. Their sole duties lay in the organization of their households and the ordering about of slaves. Unless they were Vestal Virgins, with a special place of sanctity in Roman eyes, they were excluded from any kind of public position. Murderous women like the emperor Nero's mother Agrippina were an abomination and foreign women with power – like Cleopatra herself or the Icenian queen Boudicca in Britannia in the far west – were regarded with horror.

Ptolemy II and Arsinoe established the Ptolemaia, a vast festival held every four years, which had Olympic connotations and was both to honour the memory of Alexander and to worship the god Dionysus. Drinking and feasting were the order of the day and eyewitnesses tell of processions of 80,000, with elephants and giraffes laden with exotic imports from Africa and Asia. Huge statues of gods, Greek and Egyptian, were part of these processions, with moving fountains of wine and even an 80-foot-high gold phallus to symbolize the fertility of both the Niles and the Ptolemies.

These were fabulous years for the Ptolemies and their extraordinary wealth was real. Strict laws created taxes on everything from grain to papyrus, and the colossal revenue to the royal family was collected and recorded by a highly efficient and competent civil service that only Rome would surpass 300 years later. The economy was, of course, based on agriculture and slavery, but this was the norm in the ancient world and it would be 2,000 years before anybody seriously thought of an alternative system. The money was spent on making the Egyptian army and, more especially, the navy the largest and most impressive in the world. The Ptolemies also spent a fortune on the shrines of the gods throughout their lands. At the time, this was seen as essential as the gods were all-powerful and must be appeased with lavish presents. In terms of human psychology, it kept the priests happy and in Ptolemaic Egypt and in many states since, the mood was essentially theocratic – the Ptolemies themselves were gods and the priesthood, huge and influential, worshipped them as such.

Trade brought Egypt into contact with the then unimportant city of Rome on the Tiber and the first embassy sent there in 273 marked the official start of a symbiotic relationship that would end fatally for Egypt and for Cleopatra.

Culture for the Ptolemies reached its zenith in the Museion. So used are we to these buildings as collections of old artefacts that we have forgotten its original meaning. It was the home of the muses, where all things cultural were celebrated and the amazing building in Alexandria had laboratories, lecture halls, gardens and even a zoo. At its centre was the legendary library, with its 120,000 scrolls (books) on every topic under the sun. In an extraordinarily ambitious endeavour, successive Ptolemies tried to amass all the world's knowledge under their own control, which, had it worked, would have been the ultimate in 'Big Brotherdom'.

The combination of Greek and Egyptian scholars working for the Ptolemies meant that complex histories of both countries were compiled and stored, including decrees sent out in both languages by Ptolemy V, which resulted in the survival of the Rosetta Stone, that enabled scholars of later centuries to decipher ancient hieroglyphs. Priest-physicians carried out vivisection on humans – usually criminals from the royal prisons – discovering the function of arteries, the heart and brain centuries before scientists in the West. Under Ptolemy III, scholars worked out the circumference of the earth and even invented a calendar of 365¼ days.

As each Ptolemy and his wife died, a new shrine or temple was built, each more lavish than the last, enabling the Alexandrians to claim yet more divinity for their dead rulers. Arsinoe II who died at the age of forty-six in 270 was declared the counterpart of the ancient Egyptian gods Osiris, Ra, Ptah and above all Sobek, the crocodile-god. At

Mendes, in rituals where Arsinoe was worshipped, one eyewitness was the historian Herodotus who calmly observed 'a goat tupped a woman in full view of everyone – a most surprising event'.[16] It is not clear whether he was referring to the act itself or to the presence of the audience!

The Ptolemies were polygamous and they took mistresses, too, although the Romans dismissed the minor wives as concubines by the time of Caesar's invasion – again, such practice did not conform to Roman tradition. Ptolemy II died in 246, so grossly obese for the last years of his life that he had to be carried everywhere by litter and spent hours looking enviously out of his window at everybody else moving about.

Ptolemy III, who succeeded him, married his cousin Berenice, confirming the fact that Egypt extended as far west as today's Tunisia. He also went to war with the Seleucids in Syria and reached as far as Babylon where Alexander had died over a century earlier. The couple were popular and successful, given the nickname Euergetes, the benefactors, and they produced six children. By the time of his death in 222, Ptolemy presided over a vast empire that looked unassailable. Then, family issues kicked in. In accordance with tradition, the widowed Berenice made her son Ptolemy IV co-regent. It may have given Ptolemy Philopator (Father-loving) ideas above his station or it may not have been enough for him because he had his mother and all but one of his siblings murdered. The one allowed to live was fourteen-year-old Arsinoe III whom Ptolemy later married.

Behind the scenes, the king's mistress, Agathoclea, was the real power in the land, while Ptolemy pursued women and wine in equal measure. Any opponents to this vicious regime, such as the Spartan Cleomenes living in exile at

Ptolemy's court, were killed, the man's flayed body exhibited to the mob as a warning.

Attempts by the Seleucids to take back parts of their empire grabbed by the earlier Ptolemies failed at the battle of Raphia in June 217 and Ptolemy Philopator probably read this as a sign from the gods. Antiochus the Great, king of Syria, had a massive mixed force of cavalry and infantry as well as 102 Indian elephants. Ptolemy used smaller African elephants but they refused to face their pachyderm opponents and ran.[17] Antiochus chased after them with his cavalry while Ptolemy's infantry held firm and won the day. He now called himself the new Dionysus and had himself tattooed with the god's symbolic ivy leaves. He also, like all the Ptolemies, associated himself with Alexander and he was responsible for building the astonishing tomb (Soma) in Alexandria, which was another wonder of the world. It may have had a pyramid roof in the Egyptian style and the gold sarcophagus inside was a fitting tribute to the greatest general who had ever lived. The Ptolemies and their principal wives were laid to rest alongside him.

But honouring the dead was not enough to hold a bitterly unpopular regime together. There were few popular risings in Egypt and nothing to equate with the three generations of slave revolts in Roman territory that culminated with that of the gladiator Spartacus in the year of Cleopatra's birth. From 207, however, the priests of Karnak had had enough of Ptolemy Philopator's excesses and put forward their own home-grown pharaoh as a rival – Herwennefer of Thebes. At the height of the chaos that followed, Ptolemy died: whether through natural causes (he was almost certainly an alcoholic) or murder is unknown. There is no doubt about Arsinoe III, however – her courtiers killed her, and the couple's six-year-old son became Ptolemy V.

The real power in the land was Agathoclea, but her mother, Oenanthe, had been Ptolemy III's mistress in her day and a bloody coup between followers of these two (neither of whom had any right to rule) ended with Agathoclea and other family members being dragged to the Gymnasion and torn apart by the mob. The Greek historian Polybius wrote 'some bit them, some stabbed them, others cut out their eyes … For a terrible savagery accompanies the angry passions of the people who live in Egypt.'[18] It would be interesting to find out exactly what nationality this mob was; after all, only one-fifth of Alexandria was actually Egyptian.

Under attack again from the Seleucids, who probably got wind of the disaster at the court of Ptolemy, the boy king moved south, to the ancient Egyptian capital of Memphis. The rebellion against him was put down, the ringleaders clubbed to death with stone maces at the coronation of the new king, who gave himself the title Ptolemy V Epiphanes, the Revealed. It was the decrees written now, to reveal a new birth of harmony between Greek and Egyptian gods, that are written on the Rosetta Stone.

The Seleucid king Antiochus settled for a marriage alliance rather than the more risky invasion, and at seventeen, Ptolemy was married to Antiochus' ten-year-old daughter Cleopatra who became the first of that name in the family. This girl, known as the Syrian, was the only example of 'foreign' blood to enter the Ptolemy family throughout their 300-year reign, making a nonsense of those today who claim that Cleopatra VII ('our' Cleopatra) was black.

With invasion averted and internal revolt put down (Herwennefer was captured but pardoned for the sake of harmony), all should have been well. Ptolemy V lost popularity, however, increasing taxation for foreign wars. He was murdered by his generals in 180. He was the first Ptolemy to be mummified in accordance with pharaonic tradition.

Cleopatra now named her six-year-old son Ptolemy VI Philomater (Mother-loving) as co-regent and went on to become one of the most popular queens of Egypt. Her death at twenty-eight was of natural causes and it is grim testimony to the Ptolemies' way of doing things that we have to remark on this. Ptolemy Philomater, now about ten, was married to his older sister Cleopatra II and war was resumed with the Seleucids. Their king, Antiochus IV, took Thebes and declared himself co-regent with Ptolemy and Cleopatra.

On 30 July 168 Rome made the first incursion into Graeco-Egyptian affairs. Rome was fighting the third war against Macedonia at the time and needed peace in Egypt to ensure there would be no support from that quarter, perhaps in a nostalgic memory of Alexander. A delegation under Caius Popillius Laenas took a note from the senate to Antiochus demanding that he pull out of Egypt. In accordance with diplomatic tradition – and common sense – Antiochus asked for time to think about it. Laenas drew his sword and scratched a circle in the sand around the invader-king, telling him he couldn't leave it until he had given the Romans an answer. Antiochus backed down. This gung-ho action seems the stuff of fiction, but it did wonders for Rome's military reputation and we have to admire Laenas for his sangfroid; his tiny delegation must have been outnumbered hundreds to one. What it meant for the future was that Rome would never be far away.

To make life even more confusing for historians today, there was now a three-way rule among the Ptolemies, similar to, but much cosier than, the triumvirates the Romans would establish in Cleopatra VII's time. Ptolemy Philomater continued to rule with his elder sister but a younger brother, also called Ptolemy, joined them as Ptolemy VIII. This three-way split was almost bound to fail and did, Ptolemy VI running to Rome for help to get 'his' kingdom back after being deposed by the other two. The upshot was that Ptolemy VI and Cleopatra II continued to rule in Egypt while Ptolemy VIII governed Cyrenia.

So far, so complicated, but it gets worse. Ptolemy VI and Cleopatra II effectively ignored Ptolemy VIII who had gone so far in crawling to Rome that he left all he owned to the city of the seven hills in his will. The royal couple produced Ptolemy VII as their heir and when his father was killed in a fall from his horse, the boy was made co-regent with Cleopatra II.

Re-enter Ptolemy VIII, known as Physcon (the Fat-bellied). All the Ptolemies were obese, but Physcon must have been extremely large to merit the Alexandrian nickname. He revelled in the image as a sign of wealth and opulence and invaded Egypt to claim what he saw as his rightful heritage. In a scene straight out of a horror movie, Ptolemy VII was murdered at the wedding feast of Physcon and Cleopatra II, the boy literally dying in his mother's arms. A 'night of the long knives' followed, in which any potential opposition to Physcon was removed by assassination or exile. The Alexandrians might have ridiculed Physcon behind his huge back and the Romans laughed at him when they saw him waddle to meet a delegation in 139, but officially he called himself Euergetes, the Benefactor. Most of the benefaction went to Egypt as, during his reign, Physcon promoted native Egyptians into court positions and officially recognized the power of the priests of Thebes and Memphis. One of his sons was called Ptolemy Memphites to underline the Egyptian-ness of the line. Cleopatra was happy to continue this tradition.

As soon as was expedient, Physcon removed Cleopatra II and married her daughter, Cleopatra III, who now became, in men's minds, the living Isis. Cleopatra II's popularity, however, forced Physcon into another three-way government, the two Cleopatras being officially referred to as 'the wife' and 'the sister' to avoid confusion. Cleopatra III became the mother of Ptolemies IX and X and of the three Cleopatras Tryphaena, IV and Selene.

Again the threesome collapsed, Cleopatra II forcing Physcon out in a palace coup, and this led to open warfare backed by her Jewish troops. In 132, Physcon wobbled his way to safety in Cyprus where he had Cleopatra's son Memphites murdered. The boy's mutilated remains were sent back to his mother in a jar. Once again, Physcon invaded, burning his enemies alive in the courtyard of the Gymnasion, but internal revolts would not let him resume rule by himself and the unlikely threesome was back in place.

A psychiatrist would have a field day with the Ptolemies and would not be remotely surprised by the actions of Cleopatra II's eldest daughter Thea. She now ruled in Syria, having been married to three Seleucid kings who all predeceased her, and tried to kill her own son first by firing an arrow at him and then by poisoning his wine. In a scene that Shakespeare may have stolen for *Hamlet*, the boy, Antiochus VIII Grypus (the Hook-nosed) forced his mother to quaff the goblet instead.

Against all the odds, Physcon died in his bed in June 116, leaving Cyrenia to his eldest son, Ptolemy Apion. Egypt and Cyprus went to Cleopatra III and her choice of son – Ptolemy IX – who would rule with her. So once again two Cleopatras ruled together, joined by Ptolemy IX Soter Lathyrus (Chickpea the Saviour), who wore his hair long like Alexander.

On the death of Cleopatra II, Cleopatra III became the Female Horus and when the historian Pansanius wrote that 'we know of none of the kings so hated by his mother' he was talking about the relationship between her and Chickpea. Her eldest daughter Cleopatra Tryphaena was married off to Grypus and the next, Cleopatra IV, married Antiochus IX. Since Grypus and Antiochus were half-brothers locked in a deadly war with each other, it followed that the sisters became bitter enemies too. The upshot here was that Tryphaena had Cleopatra IV murdered in the temple of Apollo, her hands hacked off as she clung, screaming, to the god's statue.

In Egypt, yet another three-way government resulted – Cleopatra III, her hated son Chickpea and the remaining daughter/sister Cleopatra Syrene. Using Chickpea's absence from Alexandria as an excuse, Cleopatra III claimed that he had tried to kill her (which would hardly be surprising) and replaced him with her youngest son, Ptolemy X, who took the *nom du roi* of Alexander and even borrowed the conqueror's helmet from the Soma to emphasize the point, complete with elephant skin and ram's horns. Cleopatra III became the most despised of the queens of that name. She gave herself five personal cults and sent hit men after Chickpea, who had fled for his life to Cyprus. The Alexandrians called her Cocce, the scarlet one, a euphemism for vagina.

The war between mother and son ended with the death of Cleopatra III, perhaps murdered by her 'loyal' son Ptolemy Alexander, who by now was far too fat to embody his namesake in any meaningful sense. Alexandrians called him, with contempt, Cocce's child, but the Egyptians loved him after he let his sister marry into the Memphis priesthood.

Ptolemy Alexander himself married his niece Berenice III who (no doubt to confuse us still further) took the honoured name of Cleopatra. The legend ran in Egypt that stone-masons left cartouches on their work blank because of the rapid turnover of rulers.

Rome was now at the gates of Egypt, extending their power with Ptolemy Appion's blessing over Cyrenia in 96. Ptolemy Alexander was overthrown by his army and fled to his sister Selene for safety. With a mercenary army of Syrians he invaded Egypt and committed the ultimate sacrilege by melting down Alexander the Great's gold sarcophagus and replacing it with glass. The gold was used to pay his unre-liable troops. His death in a naval battle with the Alexandrians saw the return of Chickpea.

All Egyptian politics from now on took place under the shadow of Rome. Not content with stealing Ptolemy's eagle emblem for their own and becoming a major buyer of Egyptian corn, the Republic now claimed that Ptolemy X Alexander had left Egypt to Rome in his will, as had Physcon before him. Rome had its own problems in the early first century BC and for now Chickpea ruled with Cleopatra-Berenice until his death in 81. Now Rome acted, sending Ptolemy XI Alexander II to rule alongside Berenice. The Alexandrians called him Pareisactus, the usurper, which seemed to say it all. Within eighteen days, the usurper had his stepmother-wife murdered and an appalled citizenry dragged him to the Gymnasion where the mob tore him to pieces. It was a grim action replay of Berenice II and Arsinoe III in 203.

Now the direct, legitimate line of Alexander came to an end. The Alexandrians ignored Rome's bullying and elected their own Ptolemy as ruler. This was Ptolemy XII, the ille-gitimate son of Ptolemy IX, and he came to be known as

Auletes, the Piper.[19] He married his sister Cleopatra Tryphaena in January 79 and they became the 'father-loving gods' and the 'brother-and-sister-loving gods', which continued to please the traditionalist Egyptians. He also called himself the new Dionysus and played his pipe in the revels held in honour of the drunken god.

The couple's first child, Berenice IV was born some time between 80 and 75 but after 69 we hear of only one daughter, 'our' Cleopatra, the last of the pharaohs.

5

CLEOPATRA THE WISE

ALEXANDRIA, 69

Bearing in mind how iconic Cleopatra has become over the centuries and how widely known, we have almost no knowledge of her birth or early life.

She was probably born in 69 BC, but it may have been 70. She was probably born in Alexandria, in the royal palaces there, but we cannot be sure. We have no clear idea who her mother was (which is where the current controversy over the black Cleopatra comes in – see Chapters 18 and 19), who attended her birth and what form the birth actually took.

The problem arises because of our lack of day-to-day knowledge of Ptolemy Auletes' court. We know that Alexandria and the Ptolemies always lay slightly outside Egyptian culture and not part of it. There had been a sort of intermarriage of the gods' pantheon and an elevation of the native priesthood that would reach its height under Cleopatra, but in important matters like the birth of a princess, which culture's wisdom would be followed? It was probably Greek, but we cannot preclude the Egyptian.

In ancient Egypt[20] signs of pregnancy included changes to skin pigmentation and eye colour. A pregnant woman would invariably have a cold back but a hot neck. Her urine could be used to detect the sex of the foetus by sprinkling it on wheat and barley grains. If the wheat germinated first, the child would be female, if vice versa, a boy. All fertility was, of course, associated with the gods. Bes, the dwarf-god, was linked with childbirth, but so were Taweret and Hathor. We have met Hathor before. There were seven or nine versions of this goddess so that she has been likened to fairy godmothers. At Cleopatra's birth house at Armant, they are shown as beautiful young women and they appeared at a child's birth to foretell its future. Taweret is universally shown as a pregnant hippopotamus, with huge breasts and standing on her hind legs. She holds a roll of papyrus and is linked with suckling as well as vengeance.

Bes, although appearing at birth, was essentially a marriage-god. He is facially repellent, which is odd for a deity so concerned with female beauty. In bas-reliefs, where most figures, human and divine, are shown in profile, Bes is full face, grimacing at us. The image has been found carved on scent bottles, rouge boxes and mirror handles; it is likely that Cleopatra owned several of them. He gave protection against nightmares and brought sweet sleep. Phalluses made of clay from the Nile were placed in temples as gifts to all these gods.

Once Cleopatra's mother, whoever she was, had conceived, if the pharaonic systems were followed, the gestation would take 271 days. During this time, prayers were said regularly and mixtures of honey and wine were taken to prevent miscarriage. Descriptions and depictions of actual childbirth are rare in Egypt. Midwives rather than doctors assisted and the mother-to-be usually squatted, sometimes on special 'birthing bricks', which are shown in the hieroglyph for birth itself. By the time of the Ptolemies, high-born women gave birth in special delivery rooms next to temples to get the utmost help from the gods. Cleopatra's at Armant is a physical reminder of these, with the shrine of the war-god Montu next door.

Various remedies helped with the pain of childbirth and speeded up delivery. Saffron and beer (probably with the accent on the beer!) was given to reduce labour pains. Localized trauma to the vagina was eased by smearing a compound of juniper berries and pine-tree resin between the legs, and prayers were offered to Isis and her child Horus and to Hathor – 'Rejoicing, rejoicing in Heaven! Birth-giving is accelerated! Come to me, Hathor, my mistress, in my fine pavilion, in this happy hour.'

Much of this information comes from pharaonic tombs and other records nearly 2,000 years before Cleopatra was born, but in the ancient world, scientific change was extremely slow, especially when, among native Egyptians, the pantheon of gods had not changed at all and everybody went along with whatever worked.

On the other hand, it may be that Cleopatra's birth took place under the Greek tradition of the Ptolemies themselves. Hippocrates, often called the father of medicine, writing in the century before Alexander, had ideas just as spurious as those of the ancient Egyptians. In relation to the sex of a child, a mother expecting a girl would be pale; if a boy she would be ruddy and healthy. In the womb, a male child lay to the right, a female to the left. In ancient Greece, all city states except Sparta tended to ignore their female babies. Breast-feeding mothers of boys were given twice as much wine, beer and grain as those nursing girls. Plato believed that pregnancy should occur between the ages of sixteen and twenty and Aristotle (Alexander's tutor) thought that a law should be passed forcing pregnant women to walk every day to the temple to pray for a safe delivery. Artemis (the Roman's Diana) was the goddess particularly associated with menstruation and childbirth, as she was linked with the early deaths of women, hit by her arrow. Deaths of mothers during pregnancy and of babies themselves were grimly common throughout the ancient world. The fact that (as far as we know) all four of Cleopatra's own children were healthy is in itself something of a record.

If we know nothing about Cleopatra's origins, we know at least who her siblings were. Berenice IV was her elder sister, the daughter of Auletes and Cleopatra V Tryphaena. The Romans would claim later that she was Auletes' only legitimate child. Arsinoe was the sister born between 69 and 65 and again we have no idea who her mother was. The boys, both called Ptolemy, were born in 61 and 59 and again, their mother is unknown. It is possible that all four children – Cleopatra, Arsinoe and the two Ptolemies – had the same mother, but we cannot know.

'Don't hesitate,' a grandmother wrote to her grand-daughter in the 180s, 'to name the little one "Kleopatra", your little daughter.'[21] The name was Macedonian, not Egyptian, and meant 'renowned in her ancestry'. She was the seventh Cleopatra of the Ptolemies and the name appears thirty-three times altogether in ancient sources.

If we know nothing about Cleopatra's birth, we are almost as much in the dark about her childhood. Clearly all the children of the Ptolemies were born with figurative silver spoons in their mouths, used to luxury and waited on hand and foot by an army of slaves. But we also know that the Ptolemies made little distinction between their children in terms of gender and education. Arsinoe and Cleopatra would have received exactly the same tuition as their younger brothers and that meant the Museion with the finest library in the world.

We have no record of who actually taught Cleopatra (it was probably her brother's tutor, the eunuch Theodotus) but the Museion was famous for its Greek and Egyptian philosophers, like Philostratus and the astronomer Sosigenes. Ironically, bearing in mind how Cleopatra became the arch-enemy of Rome, she would have spoken the same literal and metaphorical language as her later opponents – Greek. Her education would not have been very different from that of Caesar, Mark Antony or Octavian. The work was hard, with the alphabet and poetry to master, lines to be learned. She learned Homer who was as revered by Cleopatra as he was by Alexander – his works were regarded with the same awe as later Christians read the New Testament. Above all, of course, his allegories were vital to an understanding of the world not just in his time, but for all time. And (again like the Bible to Christians) every word was the truth.

She would have read Aesop's Fables, Herodotus' account of her own land, histories of the Ptolemies themselves. All this was hand-written on long papyri scrolls – which were difficult to handle – and would have been read aloud to tutors and probably class members who were her own siblings. There was no punctuation as we know it, no paragraphs, not even word breaks.

Cleopatra would have mastered the art of rhetoric or public speaking. Unlike the Romans of her generation who had to win over their assemblies and even the mob on street corners, Cleopatra's own reign had an absoluteness about it that made such speeches unnecessary. But she had to play the part for her court, her priesthood, her aristocracy and her people, both of Alexandria and of Egypt proper. So hung up are we on the woman's sexual allure that we sometimes forget she may have won over Caesar and Mark Antony with her words.

The Ptolemies were a literary family, Ptolemy Soter I writing the first biography of Alexander the Great; even the repellent Physcon wrote tracts about the birds in the royal aviaries. It is likely that Cleopatra followed this tradition, immersing herself in medicine and pharmacology. Arab sources from the seventh century AD claim that she wrote her own books on gynaecology. The Romans, quick to condemn her in the years ahead, read all kinds of evil into this. She bewitched Caesar; she bewitched Antony – it was only a miracle that her wiles didn't work on Octavian, too. And ancient Egypt had long had a tradition of poisons, spells and the occult.

Cleopatra was also a linguist of talent. She was the first Ptolemy to bother to learn Egyptian, which meant that she could not only read pharaonic missives and reliefs herself, but she could make meaningful speeches to her people, a huge step forward in the ruler–ruled relationship. The day-to-day language of Egypt was demotic; the hieroglyphs only used for architecture. She also spoke Greek, Syrian, Parthian, Medish, Ethiopian, Troglodyte, Aramaic and

Hebrew, making her a bluestocking of epic proportions. In later years, dealing with other client kings of Rome in the helter-skelter of international politics, this skill would prove highly important. One language ominously missing from her girlhood repertoire was Latin, in that Plutarch does not mention it. She would have spoken to cultured Romans in Greek. She was described as Cleopatra Thea (Augusta in Latin), the Wise, and as Theosebia, Scribe of the Gods, a reminder that literacy and education were god-given.

But if Cleopatra lived a sheltered, idyllic life surrounded by her books and her philosopher-tutors, all that would be shattered in 58 when she was eleven years old. Throughout his reign, Auletes had been forced to be a 'friend of Rome', in effect buying off invasion with huge outpourings of cash. Seizing any excuse to expand, the greedy Republic, headed now by Pompey, Caesar and Crassus (see Chapter 6), accused Auletes' brother Ptolemy of helping pirates against Roman shipping in the Mediterranean and grabbed the Cyprus treasury from him.

Once again the Alexandrians intervened in what they saw as their right to oust an unsatisfactory ruler. In a sense, the Alexandrian mob was as vocal and powerful as that of Rome two centuries later. Since Auletes had not gone to his brother's aid, but stood meekly by while the Romans claimed yet another scalp, they kicked the Piper out of Alexandria and called the exiled Cleopatra V Tryphaena to co-rule with Auletes' eldest daughter, Berenice IV. An Athenian epitaph says that Auletes sailed to Rhodes with 'one of his daughters'. This cannot be Berenice, who stayed as joint pharaoh, and Arsinoe was an infant, so the daughter had to be Cleopatra. It is always dangerous to trust one historical source, and some historians like Adrian

Goldsworthy don't really buy what happened next, but if Cleopatra went on a royal progress with her father on the eve of womanhood, it would explain a great deal about the ease with which she entered the world of realpolitik in her own right five years later. If she stayed behind, continuing her cloistered education, who was the daughter referred to in the epitaph?

The island of Rhodes was an ally of the Ptolemies and Isis was worshipped there. Joann Fletcher imagines the young Cleopatra seeing the Colossus of Rhodes, another wonder of the world now flattened by an earthquake, and being hugely impressed. This is possible, but Auletes had a less pleasant encounter. Marcus Porcinus Cato, on his way to Cyprus to organize the Roman takeover, insisted that Auletes came to him rather than the other way round and interviewed him sitting on the toilet. This seems amazingly high-handed, a mere politician dictating terms to what today would be called an emperor. It may have made Auletes feel better had he known that Cato was in disgrace himself. He had fallen foul of Caesar in Rome and the Cyprus job was a sort of short exile. He was not a popular man, wallowed in nostalgia for the Rome of his great-grandfather Cato 'the Censor' and hired his second wife out to the lawyer Quintus Hortensius: hardly an example of the famous Roman 'virtue'.

Happier times waited for the royal father and daughter in Athens where the Ptolemies were regarded as gods, and there would have been endless speeches and feasting. Then they sailed for Rome. As we shall see in Chapter 6, by 58 almost all of the old empire in the west that belonged to Alexander had been taken by the Romans in their drive to master the world, and in Italy they were met by the general who most modelled himself on the conqueror – Pompey, who called himself 'the Great' and wore a Macedonian haircut. He lent the Ptolemies his beautiful villa to the south of Rome during their stay.

Auletes and Cleopatra spent several months in Rome, wheeling and dealing with the notoriously difficult senate and sparring with the 'three pillars of the world' – Pompey, Crassus and Caesar – each of whom had an ego and an ambition bigger than Egypt itself. The wrangling of these months will be described later but they left Auletes broke and he travelled east to Ephesus, in modern Turkey. Here was another wonder of the world: the great temple dedicated to Artemis but linked for ever with Alexander. Auletes had the temple decorated with a huge pair of doors made from ivory. Broke as he was, it was important to be seen to be appeasing the gods.

It was while the royals were at Ephesus that news reached them of the death of Cleopatra V Tryphaena. Berenice IV, now ruling alone, panicked. For centuries, the Egyptian pattern of government had been a co-rulership, but her little brothers were too young and she felt she could not govern Egypt alone. Various attempts to find a family member who would do were blocked by the Roman governor of Syria, Aulus Gabinius, who was only too happy to be difficult on Auletes' behalf as long as the man continued to line his purse.

An obscure Seleucid claimant was found, whom the Alexandrians called scornfully Cybiosictes, the Salt-fish Seller, but Berenice didn't like him and had him strangled days after their marriage. She found a replacement in Archelaos, who claimed to be a son of Mithridates VI, king of Pontus, whose family had been at war with Rome for generations. By that time, however, all bets were off because Pompey, angling for control of Egypt for himself, ordered his subordinate Gabinius to put the Piper back on the throne.

It took a Roman army to do it and the officer commanding the cavalry was Mark Antony. According to legend, he fell in love with the fourteen-year-old Cleopatra at first sight; in reality, he probably never noticed her. Antony took the city of Pelusium on the eastern tributary of the Nile delta and marched to Alexandria where Auletes had his own daughter Berenice and her followers slaughtered. Only Antony stopped him from restaging the ritual dismemberment in the Gymnasion for which the Ptolemies were infamous.

On 31 May 52 a great ceremony was held in Alexandria. All four of Auletes' children were on display; the eldest, Cleopatra, now sixteen, was officially called Thea Philopator, Father-loving Goddess, and she sat beside the Piper as his co-ruler. It was the thirteenth year of his reign and the first of hers and on the face of it, it must have looked to witnesses that here was just another joint government of the Ptolemies, not unlike those that had gone on for nearly 300 years.

Rome saw it differently.

BOOK THREE:
WINGS OF THE EAGLE

6

TIBER, FATHER TIBER

ROME, 753

Cities and institutions like Rome always have a colourful creation story attributed to them; in the case of Rome there are two. The first says that the city was founded by the twins Romulus and Remus, the children of Rhea Silvia and the great god of war, Mars. Abandoned by their mother, the boys were found, suckled and raised by a she-wolf. The statue commemorating this stood on the Capitoline Hill in Rome when Cleopatra was born, and the orator Marcus Tullius Cicero wrote that it was struck by lightning, probably when Cleopatra was four. The other story links Rome with the mythical Trojan War and has the Trojan prince Aeneas founding 'New Troy' on the banks of the Tiber in central Italy after fleeing the flames of his home somewhere in Asia Minor.

What is interesting is that both stories deal with loss and violence – constants in the ancient world. Romulus battered Remus to death with a spade when he jestingly jumped over a ditch of the city whose foundations he had just dug – the sort of familial slaughter that was almost *de rigueur* among the Ptolemies. Aeneas was a war refugee, escaping from a slaughter that, according to Homer, saw Trojan women raped and babies carried on the spear-point of conquering Greek heroes. Similar scenes must have accompanied the whirlwind eleven-year campaign of Alexander.

The reality, of course, is different. The Latin tribe who became the Romans were one among many. They settled on the Palatine Hill above the Tiber about 1000 BC. They were herdsmen; scattered archaeology has revealed the bones of cattle, sheep, goats and pigs. The seven hills over which their settlements spread were really a series of rocky valleys through which the Tiber's tributaries splashed, leading to the dismal marshes that were home to teeming millions of mosquitoes, which continued to keep the death rate high for centuries. Their houses were wooden structures, circular or rectangular, filled in with wattle and clay between the uprights. The Tiber not only provided a water supply, but fish were abundant and the river was easily wide and deep enough to accommodate even the largest ships of the ancient world, so trade could develop.

In the cliché of the older history books, Italy was a 'geographical expression' before its final unity in 1861. For the first eight centuries of Rome's life, its inhabitants were living in a sort of tribal jungle in which social Darwinism was a reality. To the south, in Sicilia and Campania, the Greeks dominated with their scholarship, their democracy and their libertine ways. For centuries, Capua, one of their major cities, vied with Rome as the power house of Italy. To the north, the Etruscans held sway as far as the Alps. They were exotic craftsmen and brilliant traders and every bit as greedy and expansionist as the Romans became.

Early in the seventh century BC, the Etruscans came south, forcing the Romans and other former enemies to band together for survival. The kings of Rome in these years have folkloric names and, like Romulus himself, almost a god-like figure already, they were depicted as divine. Tullus Hostilius, for example, c.673–c.641, was a warmonger on a colossal scale. The historian Titus Livius (Livy), a contemporary of Cleopatra, summed him up when he wrote: 'When [Hostilius] fell ill himself, the long sickness changed his mind…his proud spirit was broken, so that he seemed to have become another man.'[22]

It didn't help in the advent of the Etruscans that Rome could never quite bury the hatchet with all her former enemies. The Sabines, inland from Rome, were not finally defeated until 290. The Aequians along the River Anio continued fighting until their absorption into Rome forty years later. An earlier enemy, whom Shakespeare was fascinated by in *Coriolanus*, were the Volscians who seem to have been completely Romanized by 304. Over time, Roman resistance to Etruria became offence rather than defence.

In the days of the kings, Roman society was divided by tribe. There were three, each responsible for providing soldiers in times of war. Each tribe was divided into ten *curia* (houses) who advised the king on day-to-day matters, but had no power themselves. Alongside this, a class structure was also developing and it was very polarized by Cleopatra's time. The patricians were the wealthy, a military class who came to dominate politics, trade, everything.

Three of the major Roman protagonists in Cleopatra's story – Caesar, Pompey and Octavius – all came from this class. Under them came the plebeians, the ordinary people. According to the first/second-century AD Greek historian Plutarch (a very important source for Cleopatra), the plebeians were organized by the second (and most peaceful) of Rome's kings, Numa Pompilius, with a degree of sophistication unknown in the ancient world. 'He divided the craftsmen according to their trades – flute-players, goldsmiths, carpenters, dyers, shoemakers, leather-dressers, potters and workers in copper and brass.'[23]

The mud huts on the Palatine became large, solid buildings made of brick or stone. Tarquinius Priscus (the Old) set up an ambitious public works scheme. Stone was quarried, trees felled, plebeians laboured long and hard, their wagons groaning with building materials. Conduits and ditches were dug – the stinking malarial ditch into which all the city's effluent ran became the Cloaca Maxima (the great arsehole), which was so high and wide that a hay wagon could pass through it.

As Rome's size grew and her power became obvious, her armies proved ever more successful throughout Italy. With that power came corruption and an ever greater reliance on slave labour. In Cleopatra's day, the slave population of Rome probably outnumbered freemen four to one. The city was sitting on a potential powder-keg that could explode any minute and did in the form of Spartacus in the year of Cleopatra's birth. More pressing than the slave problem by the sixth century was the over-reaching arrogance of the kings. The reign of Tarquinius Superbus (Tarquin the Proud) tipped Rome's patience over the edge. There was no heredity in kingship but Tarquin took the throne by force with no popular backing at all. 'He accepted,' wrote Livy, 'that there was no hope of his being accepted into the hearts of his subjects, so he ruled by fear.'[24] A successful soldier and great builder, he should have been exactly what the Romans respected but the actions of his son, Sextus, provided the spark for revolution.

Spoiled and indulged, the boy was obsessed with a married woman, Lucretia, who was given a straight choice – submit to Sextus' lust or be branded a whore for having sex with a slave. Lucretia chose to live but then, racked with guilt, committed suicide (that fine, Roman end). Led by a hardliner, Lucius Junius Brutus, the city's population forced Tarquin and his son out and set up a Republic that was tottering to its own fall at the time of Cleopatra.

The government of the Republic was complicated. It was designed to prevent a return to the despotism of Tarquin but at the same time was nothing like a modern democracy nor even the original Athenian form of that style of government. Service to Rome was essential – *Res Publica* meant public matters and everyone, high and low, was expected to bear responsibility. The only problem was that, anxious to avoid tyranny, various officials only held office for a year and could not stand again for a decade. Such novices were expected to control the mob (always a problem), provide bread and circuses (to keep the mob happy), feed, clothe and water the city and fight whichever enemy took the field against Rome.

The role of the *Praetor* (there were sixteen of them by Cleopatra's time) was to administer justice as a magistrate. The *Praetor Urbanus* had jurisdiction in the city limits; the *Praetor Peregrinus* kept watch on the endless stream of foreigners trickling to the magnet that was Rome. It was expecting a lot of a man that he could cope with the finer points of the Twelve Tablets of Roman Laws as well as taking the field against enemies as dangerous as, say, Hannibal the Carthaginian (see Chapter 7). Those who did well went on to become consuls; those who did not often became governors of provinces as the 'empire' spread before it even had an emperor.

The *Aedile* was responsible for supervising the various markets throughout the city, as well as maintaining the temples, aqueducts and baths. The markets, of course, were the city's lifeblood and it was here that the grain of Egypt was sold long before the two peoples recognized each other politically. Aqueducts carried water supplies from the Tiber and its tributaries and were astonishing works of engineering, a lasting complement to Roman know-how.

As far as the temples were concerned, the religion of Rome was complicated and became more so as the 'empire' grew. The pantheon of gods was passed on from that of the Greeks; only the names had changed to Romanize them – Zeus became Jupiter, Artemis was Diana, Ares turned into Mars, and so on. Cults came and went depending on the trend of the time – the Greek god Dionysus, worshipped by the Ptolemies, never really took off; Dionysus became Bacchus, a lascivious, useless drunk whose orgies were actively discriminated against in Cleopatra's time. Above all, however, the *Aedile* organized games that ran for days and commemorated the feast of one god or another. The gladiatorial contests that were a regular part of these ceremonies were immensely popular wherever the eagles flew.

The *Quaestor* was a record-keeper and controller of the treasury. He had to be at least twenty-five and to have served as an officer in the army. There were forty of these under Julius Caesar. The *Quaestor* worked hand in glove with the Censor, who held a very wide remit. Cicero described his job:

> [The Censors] shall divide citizens into tribes and list them according to wealth, age and rank. They shall assign young men to the cavalry and infantry. They shall discourage the unmarried state, guard public morality and suspend from the senate anyone guilty of improper conduct.[25]

The Censor checked the suitability of plays (in Shakespeare's England *Antony and Cleopatra* would have been checked by a similar busybody called the Master of the Revels), supervised public gardens and had the power to demote the social rank of anyone who broke the law.

Lastly, the *Pontifex Maximus* was the bridge builder between gods and men. He was not actually a religious leader, but appointed the sisterhood of the Vestal Virgins (the perfection of chaste Roman womanhood) and disciplined transgressing priests. The job was for life (unlike any political posts of the Republic) and the title was passed centuries later to the Pope.

The best known aspect of the Republic's government was the Senate, with its famous initials still found on Roman public buildings today – SPQR; *Senatus Populusque Romanus* – the Senate and the people of Rome. It was composed of about 300 men of the patrician class (women were accorded no official power under the Republic) and the image we have from various men who were there is of toga-clad politicians sitting on their curved marble seats and hurling abuse at each other. In fact, some of Rome's finest oratory came from that platform. In a clever nod to inclusivity, plebeians were allowed in from the fourth century, but in practice, only those with administrative experience could join, so that in effect, only the patricians held sway. Unlike its modern American counterpart, the senate was not actually a legislative body, but it controlled finances, tax collection and foreign policy, so its advice was always taken seriously.

Four sub-committees operated within the Senate. The *Comitia Curiata* (household assembly) represented the twenty wards of the city set up under the kings. It was a court of appeal and supervised the election of the Consuls, but by Cleopatra's day, most of its work was carried out by the *Comitia Centuriata*. This was originally made up of ex-army men but by about 200 had become largely civilian. It had 193 seats, eighty-eight of them belonging to the wealthiest patricians. It could approve laws and peace treaties, declare war and decide issues of exile, life and death. The *Comitia Tributa* was open to all citizens and elected minor officials; its powers were a throwback to the earliest days of the Republic and very limited. Finally, the *Concilium Plebis*, the People's Council, represented thirty-five outlying districts, but its decisions covered the whole city.

Like any institution as complex and powerful as Rome, it was a mass of contradiction. All Romans respected the concept of the wife and mother, but women had no political voice and prostitution was rife in every major Roman town. Millions of men, women and children toiled as slaves in the latifundia, the fields that fed Rome, and they were bought and sold as cattle. There was no law against killing a slave. Candidates for election bribed those with the vote and shamelessly made promises they could not possibly keep. Money talked – Marcus Licinius Crassus who ran Rome with Pompey and Caesar when Cleopatra was a young woman bought up so much derelict property in the city that he was given the nickname '*Dives*' – the rich one.

In reality, the story of the Roman Republic was one of powerful men vying with each other to become more powerful still. And the best way to do that was to control the army, the most formidable fighting force of the ancient world.

7

MARS VICTOR

ROME, 753

The Roman army could be defeated. In 321 the Samnites won a famous victory over them in the convoluted valleys of the Caudine Forks. Livy wrote:

> The consuls, half-naked, suffered the ignominious ordeal of being sent under the yoke. They were followed by their officers, in descending order of rank; then, one after the other, by the legions themselves, while the enemy, fully armed, stood around, hurling insults and cracking jokes.[26]

Between 71 and 69 Spartacus destroyed six different armies that Rome sent against him. Not only were they beaten at their own game, they were beaten by an army of slaves, the lowest of the low. The man who defeated them, Marcus Licinius Crassus, was only awarded an ovation by Rome, not the full-blown triumph given for victory over a conventional foreign enemy.

In the Teutoberg Forest in north Germany in AD 9, Publius Varus was completely outfought in a series of ambushes over several days. Varus himself committed suicide and his three legions, perhaps 15,000 men, were massacred.

It *could* happen, but not often. What marked Roman military conquest was the sheer tenacity of the Roman soldier. The Samnites were eventually defeated thirty years before Cleopatra's birth. Spartacus was killed in battle by Crassus in the year of her birth and 6,000 of his followers were crucified along the Appian Way into Rome as a reminder of the fate that awaited anyone who took on the city of the seven hills. The Teutoberg disaster was a mere glitch in the conquest of the southern part of Germany, which would not be wiped out for 400 years.

Rome was at war for an astonishingly long time and was the most aggressive military force in Italy. We have already seen that her armies destroyed the Sabines, the Aequians and the Volsci, and in 370 Marcus Camillus defeated the Cisalpine Gauls on the River Arno. Thirty years later Valerius Corvus destroyed Satricia, the Sabine capital. Thirty years after that, Lucius Scapula beat the Etruscans.

The army that won these victories was still a citizen army, composed of farmers who served their city voluntarily, but as the defensive battles became offensive and the campaigns were fought ever further afield, the structure of the Roman war machine had to change. What also changed was the means by which the army marched.

Think Rome – think roads. They were dug straight as arrows to cover the miles quickly – the very name miles derives from the Latin word for soldier – and they had firm surfaces and drainage ditches to allow the rainwater to run off. The Appian Way, which ran south from Rome, was the road that saw the legions of Caesar, Mark Antony and Octavius march for Egypt. It was built by the censor Appius Claudius Caecus (the Blind) as early as 312 and was originally 152 miles long, extending to the port of Brundisium later. Such roads spread the tentacles from Rome and were built wherever the legions had permanent camps.

The biggest obstacle that Rome faced outside the Italian peninsula was Carthage, the North African empire covering modern Tunisia. Rome fought Carthage three times – the Punic Wars – over a long period, which cost thousands of lives, destroyed whole tracts of countryside and almost wiped out some of Rome's most powerful families. The geographer Strabo estimated that the Poeni (the Roman name for Carthaginians – hence Punic) had a population of 700,000 and nearly 300 *colonia*, cities that made up their empire. The Carthaginians traded slaves, tin, gold, corn, bronze, iron, dyestuffs and perfumes, and they saw the islands of the Mediterranean, especially Sardinia and Corsica, as outposts of their empire.

The first Punic War focused on the sea. For twenty-three years, war-galleys grappled together in a bid for supremacy. The army sent to Sicily in 264 succeeded in taking the island, but the invasion of North Africa under Marcus Atilius Regulus fell apart when his fleet was destroyed with huge loss of life. Hamilcar Barca was unable to follow this up with a swift counter-attack and two years of sieges on Sicily itself gave the Romans time to rebuild their fleet and effectively starve the Carthaginian garrisons out. Barca surrendered, ceding Sicily permanently to Rome.

It was the second Punic War that terrified Rome because this time the fighting came to them. It produced one of the finest generals in the ancient world – Hannibal. Legend says that as a boy of nine he swore an oath to oppose Rome and spent his adult life keeping that oath. Ignoring the endless war of manoeuvre and fleets that had cost his country Sicily, he invaded Italy from the north, marching into the Po Valley with his war elephants, which terrified the Romans who had never seen anything like them before. In a whirlwind series of battles – Trebia, Lake Trasimene and above all Cannae – he put the legions to the sword. At Cannae, the consuls Gaius Terentius Varro and Lucius Aemilius Paullus drew up their battle formations of 80,000 men and attacked head-on in the usual Roman way, the legions marching in grim silence, shield to shield through Hannibal's centre of Spaniards and Celts. They realized too late that this was a Carthaginian feint and Hannibal's Numidian cavalry closed in on their flanks like a giant crab's claw. Paullus was killed along with half his command.

The problem for Hannibal was Rome itself. The city was inevitably well fortified and Quintus Fabius Maximus and Claudius Marcellus prevented Carthaginian alliances with local tribes so that Hannibal had to get his supplies from Carthage itself. Since Rome once more commanded the sea, this was a major obstacle and by 208 Rome had taken Spain from Carthage. Four years later Scipio, later named Africanus for his success, invaded Carthage itself and faced Hannibal at Zama in 202. This time the Romans were ready for the elephants and the braying of Roman trumpets seems to have unnerved the animals who were lured into cul-de-sacs of infantry and slaughtered. The treaty of Scipio brought the war to a close and Hannibal ended his days as a wandering freak before finally committing suicide.

The third Punic War was very much a mopping-up operation. It lasted for only three years and ended with the sacking of Carthage itself. An estimated 200,000 suits of armour and 3,000 siege engines found their way to Rome and the survivors of the smouldering city were sold into slavery. 'Delenda est Carthago' Cato told the Senate in 153 – 'Carthage must be destroyed' – it was and everybody breathed a sigh of relief.

In a speech to his troops before Zama, Scipio Africanus told his men they were fighting not merely to defeat Carthage, but to dominate the world. Like peoples before and after them, the Romans had a divine right, they believed, to conquer. It was a grim mindset, but it was held universally by a nation that believed implicitly in its own superiority and was prepared to go to any lengths to achieve it. Fifty years before Cleopatra's birth, the empire with no emperor extended from Iberia (Spain) in the west to Bithynia and Pontus (Turkey) in the east and included Greece and Alexander's own Macedonia.

Much of the aggression of Roman conquest came from the political system we looked at in the last chapter. Government was dominated by the elite and ambitious men at the top who followed the cursus honorum, the path of honour to the consulship if they could. There were only two consuls at any given time and they only held office for a year, so there was a need to impress and quickly. The greatest method of doing this was to be awarded a triumph for feats of arms, riding in a chariot through Rome's streets, thronged with flower-throwing fans who marvelled at the spoils taken in war and the defeated enemies dragged in chains behind the legions. Each triumph was accompanied by games and was expected to be more lavish than the last.

A rational analysis of most of the wars of conquest fought by the Romans before the birth of Christ shows a recurring pattern. Early days of each campaign were characterized by embarrassing losses and some humiliation, especially when charismatic enemies like Hamilcar, Hannibal, Vercingetorix and Arminius led their men with brilliance. It is not true to say that Rome fought every year or that her consuls always went to war. The stop-go military policy led to quiet periods in which experience was lost and the legions had to learn to fight all over again. There was a need, above all, to improve the quality and consistency of the Roman soldier; to move, in effect, from the amateur to the professional. The man generally held to be responsible for this transition is Gaius Marius who died, probably from a stroke, sixteen years before Cleopatra was born. Hugely influential though Marius was, the changes were already under way when he was a boy and were more gradual than historians used to accept.

The army recruit was increasingly a labourer, without ties to his own farmland in the latifundia, and was bound to make for an improvement. A man who is constantly worrying about his wife, children and the harvest makes a poor soldier unless he is specifically fighting to defend them. Flavius Vegetius Renatus was writing nearly 500 years after Cleopatra, but he used earlier Roman sources, including Julius Caesar, and describes a recruit of the first century BC:

> A young soldier who is chosen for the work of Mars should have alert eyes and should hold his head upright. [He] should be broad-chested with powerful shoulders and brawny arms. His fingers should be long rather than short.

He should not be pot-bellied or have a fat bottom. His calves and feet should not be flabby; instead they should be made entirely of tough sinew …smiths, carpenters, butchers and hunters of deer and wild boar are the most suitable…[27]

Old distinctions of recruitment, based on age and property ownership, disappeared and the focus of the army became the legion. In theory 6,000 strong, on campaign the unit usually mustered about 4,800 and even that could be reduced by sickness and secondment. The old sub-division of the maniple, stolen from the Greek hoplite armies of Alexander, became the cohort, of 480 men, divided into six further sub-units of eighty, commanded by a centurion. The senior officers were the tribunes, six per legion, each with a specific role. The senior centurion was the *primus pilus* (first spear), a reminder of the tactical weapons soldiers carried. Each soldier carried two spears, the javelin (*pilum*) for throwing and the *hasta* for stabbing. By Cleopatra's time, only the javelin remained. The legionary carried a short, straight, double-edged sword (*gladius*) and a *pugio* (dagger) and usually wore the overlapping breast and back plates made famous by Hollywood, the *lorica segmentata*.[28] The head was protected by a helmet with ear flaps and a neck flange for maximum protection and a large curved angular shield (*scutum*) served as both a defence mechanism and a weapon. An advancing unit would bat the enemy aside with these shields before stabbing their falling or fallen bodies with the sword.

On the battlefield the cohorts advanced in silence, in the *triplex acies* (three-line) formation, which could easily change direction and deploy in one, two or four lines. Endless training led to perfection of these tactics and most opponents, especially the Gauls and Britons, tried to smash the formations with a wild, headlong charge. This was usually ineffective and led to exhaustion and a lack of cohesion on which the legions capitalized.

The old emblems of Rome's citizen armies – the boar, the wolf, the horse – which could be found in most armies of the ancient world were replaced in the legion by the silver eagle and carried by the aquilifer with his distinctive lion or wolf-skin headdress. The eagle, of course, had been pinched by the Romans from the personal badge of Ptolemy II.

But if the heart of the new professional army was the legion, the cavalry (*alae*) were often recruited from former enemies, especially the Iberians. They were deployed on the wings of battle formations to harass the enemy and turn a retreat into a rout. The auxiliaries served as light infantrymen, in some cases being virtually indistinguishable from the legions themselves. Specialist troops were used to build roads and bridges and to fire the highly effective ballistic weapons used in siege operations. For example, when Julius Caesar reached the River Thames in the summer of 54, he had Batavian troops with him who were experts in river crossings.

The irony of the professionalization of the Roman soldier was that such men lost their sense of identification with Rome itself. They relied on their pay (and were sometimes mutinous if they didn't get it) and became intensely loyal to their unit or their commander. So popular was Caesar with his troops in Gaul that his men openly sang songs about his baldness (about which he was very sensitive) and his homosexual leanings. This might sound negative to the point of insubordination, but it was the stuff that glued armies together. The flip side of this development was that by Cleopatra's day, rivalries between politicians, like Caesar and Pompey, for example, or Mark Antony and Octavian, became bloody affairs involving whole armies of thousands of men.

8

THE CRACKS IN THE PAVEMENT

ROME, 88

The Romans may have thrown out their last king, Tarquinius Superbus, appalled by the man and everything he stood for, but they did not replace him with anything like a democracy, so that in reality a handful of Tarquin's over-mighty subjects took over and spent the next 500 years jostling each other for power. The whole system *seemed* to be held in check by the senate and the other councils we have met already, but the reality was that supremely ambitious and egotistical men fought each other for overall power. The smooth pavement that was the Roman ideal had cracks in it from the beginning. On the Ides of March 44, Julius Caesar was stabbed to death on his way into the senate by republicans who found his ambition too much to stomach; but it could be argued that the first man to plunge his dagger into the notion of the Republic was Lucius Cornelius Sulla – 'Lucky'.

An impoverished young man with skin so sensitive it was described as 'mulberries sprinkled with flour',[29] two legacies in rapid succession gave him enough money to enter politics. The way to the top in republican Rome – and it was to remain so throughout Europe for the next 2,000 years – was to attach oneself to a rising star. For Sulla, the star was Marius and he impressed against the Numidian king Jugurtha in Africa before serving against the Germanii in 104 and 103. Marius was clearly jealous of his protégé and the young *quaestor* gravitated towards Marius' rival, Quintus Lutatius Catulus. He made a political mistake in not standing as *aedile*, because whoever arranged the games was already a popular figure and Sulla's African connections could have brought some weird and wonderful animals into Rome's arena. His attempt at the praetorship foundered. Only by paying huge sums in bribes did he get the *Praetor Urbanus* job in 98.

Military successes followed against one of the trickiest of Rome's enemies, the Parthians, who had come to dominate the eastern extent of Alexander the Great's empire. Consul by 88, Sulla gave himself the official nickname 'Felix', loosely translated as lucky, but in reality blessed by fortune, a reminder that even the most hard-bitten soldiers and statesmen of the ancient world wholeheartedly believed in prophecies and auguries; their lives were driven by them, in Rome as in Egypt.

A showdown between Sulla and Marius was perhaps inevitable and the jealous Marius forced Sulla out, amid riotous scenes in the senate and fighting in the streets. Sulla himself fled but returned at the head of an army to restore order at sword point. This was a low point in Roman history – Roman soldiers called out to enforce discipline on their own people – and virtually all Sulla's officers refused to obey him. Promotion from the junior ranks was easily achieved and when two *praetors* were sent to Sulla to talk sense into him, he sent them back to the senate with their togas ripped and their staffs of office broken in their hands. Sulla marched on Rome and took it.

The phrase 'in denial' still lay two millennia in the future in Sulla's day but it fitted his situation perfectly. He was unpopular with most Romans, who elected a rival, Lucius Cornelius Cinna, as consul the next year and Sulla was ordered to stand trial for his crimes against the senate and the people of Rome. He simply refused to turn up and set off at the head of his army against Mithridates, the general who had snatched most of Asia Minor back from the Romans. The Greeks, in whose lands the campaign began, were uncertain who to support so Sulla burned the port of Piraeus and seriously damaged Athens, despite its almost holy reputation as the cradle of civilization. He was more than holding his own against Mithridates when news arrived of a revolt in Rome spearheaded by Marius and Cinna. Sulla's house had been burned down and his lands declared forfeit. In 85 the rebel consul made peace with Mithridates (which outraged the army) and he marched back home.

Other rebels joined him as he reached the port of Brundisium – Appius Claudius, Metellus Pius and two men who would play tangential roles in the life of Cleopatra – Marcus Licinius Crassus and Gaius Pompey. With a mixture of bluff, cunning and appalling savagery, the outnumbered Sulla fought his way to Rome's Colline Gate. Here Appius Claudius was killed and Sulla's centre driven back but

Crassus' right wing had destroyed the enemy and in a moment that no fiction writer would dare invent, he sent a messenger to Sulla to ask if his men could stand down and have their supper!

A terrified senate gave Sulla the title of dictator. The technical definition was that of a consul with exceptional powers, granted in times of emergency, including those of life and death, against whom there was no appeal. On the face of it, looking backwards, it was difficult to see how different this was from the role of the Tarquin kings and looking forward, of course, it foreshadowed the rise of the emperors. In a terrifying purge which dictators of later centuries have carried out – think Hitler and Stalin in the twentieth century – Sulla proscribed names of 500 men he saw as his enemies and therefore the enemies of Rome. Having decimated the senate he then doubled its size and packed it with his cronies. The magistracy was increased – there were now eight *praetors* and twenty *quaestors*. The power of the people's tribunes was curbed – all 'junior' assemblies had to have their decisions ratified by the senate and the senate belonged to Sulla.

The jury is still out on the dictator's next step. Having amassed unprecedented power over a three-year period, he returned Rome to the status quo in 80 with Metellus Pius and himself as joint consuls and retired from politics completely in 79. Should we see him as a former-day Oliver Cromwell, actually trying to find a better governmental system than the one he had overthrown? Hardly, because in 80 everything returned to 'normal' and only negativity had triumphed. He died in 78, having completed his memoirs, now lost to time, and left behind a nagging doubt in Rome and a yawning chasm in its pavement. The stock phrase from now on became:

'Sulla did it; why can't I?' Increasingly the real power of Rome was its army, not its senate and the man who commanded it could 'bestride the narrow world like a colossus'.

The remaining consul was Metellus Pius – the nickname means devoted, not holy in the modern sense, and the devotion was to his father who had been exiled in 99 on the order of Marius. He was *praetor* in 89 and fought effectively against the neighbouring Italian tribe, the Marsi, before a less successful campaign in Africa. His competence as a general endeared him to the army and he joined the rebel Sulla as a natural opponent of Marius. As a reward, Sulla made Metellus *Pontifex Maximus* with its priestly overtones, and as proconsul and consul fought a bitter war against the rebel Sertorius in Spain. He retired shortly before Cleopatra's birth when her father Auletes was anxious to court Roman military power and the stage was set for the last titanic struggle in Roman affairs that would lead to the deaths of Pompey the Great, Julius Caesar, Mark Antony and Cleopatra and the rise of the emperors under Augustus.

Marcus Licinius Crassus was played with all the hauteur of a Roman patrician by Laurence Olivier in the film *Spartacus*. What did not come out in that portrayal was the man's avarice, which appalled his patrician peers. He made a point of buying up property cheaply all over Rome so that he could sell it at an obscene profit. When Auletes went to Rome to bribe various officials, it is highly likely that Crassus was more than interested. He bought people with the same ease that he bought property and was popular among Romans of the lower classes, taking on pro bono cases in the law courts.

When Cleopatra was born, the Thracian gladiator slave Spartacus was looting Italian towns at will. Five armies sent against him were destroyed and the sixth was commanded by Crassus, by now *propraetor*. He took six legions – an unprecedentedly large army, especially against slaves – and defeated Spartacus somewhere south of Rome. It was in the mopping-up operations of this campaign that Gaius Pompey arrived. He magnanimously acknowledged Crassus' victory, but overstepped the mark perhaps by suggesting that he had made sure a similar revolt would never happen again. Pompey's father was a highly dubious politician and so prone to changing sides between Marius and Sulla that when he died of plague, his body was dragged from its tomb by the mob and torn apart in scenes usually reserved for the Ptolemies in Alexandria. Sulla's arrival at Brundisium brought Pompey with three legions raised at his own cost to support him. His early military successes as a dashing cavalry commander went to his head a little, especially when Sulla hailed him as *imperator* (conquering general, which later became synonymous with emperor). It was now that Pompey began to compare himself with Alexander the Great, cutting his blond hair in the style of the Macedonian conqueror.

While Crassus looked on bemused in 82, Pompey demanded a triumph in Rome for his defeat of the Marian exiles Carbo in Sicily and Ahenobarbus[30] in Africa. Roman protocol demanded that triumphs were only given to those who had held public office and Pompey had not. Even so, he would not be dissuaded and the day went ahead. Somehow typical of Pompey's brashness, his elephant-hauled chariot got stuck on a city gate and he became something of a laughing stock.

Manoeuvring for position as Sulla's blue-eyed boy, Pompey divorced his wife Antistia and married the dictator's stepdaughter, Aemilia. When she died in childbirth,

Pompey married Mucia Tertia, another member of the same family, and she produced a son, Gnaeus, in 79. For the next two years, Pompey fought against Sertorius in Spain, although most of the successful campaigning was done by Metellus. Returning to Italy for the end of the Spartacus campaign, Pompey hurried himself through the usual political process and stood with Crassus as consul in the year of Cleopatra's birth. The pair were hardly friends – Crassus the aloof patrician and Pompey the boy-general (although by now, of course, he was thirty-six) were not a match made in heaven.

It was now that Pompey officially added the nickname Magnus – the Great – and he had to earn his sobriquet. Rome's navy was never as accomplished as its army, and the pirates of Cilicia (northern Turkey today) were able to out-row and out-sail the Roman fleets and raid coastal towns at will. When Cleopatra was three, the senate unleashed Pompey against the pirates and in a lightning forty-day campaign, he penned them in, took 90 ships, 20,000 prisoners and umpteen chests of stolen loot. An ecstatic senate voted to extend Pompey's powers and ordered him against Mithridates VI Eupator, the king of Pontus, who was the greatest obstacle to Rome's expansion in the east. Sulla had beaten the man in 84, as had Lucius Lucullus three years later, but, like a bad denarius, he kept turning up.

Once again, Pompey was indeed great, defeating Mithridates before turning on Tigranes of Armenia. This man, an ally of Mithridates, used the grand Parthian title of 'king of kings', but was captured and obliged to pay Pompey a huge ransom before the Roman went on to invade Syria and Judaea. Mithridates finally committed suicide in the Crimea in 63, having fought Rome for thirty years.

In 62, when the little Cleopatra was probably studying with her Greek philosophers in the great library at Alexandria, Pompey celebrated his third triumph in Rome. This one was so spectacular that the column of troops, captured prisoners of war and booty took days to march through the streets. Impressing the rabble was one thing; working for stability in Roman politics was another, and Pompey clashed with too many important members of the senate for his own good. He divorced Mucia Tertia on the unprovable grounds of infidelity, thus alienating her powerful family, and found himself at odds not only with Lucullus but with Gaius Porcius Cato, tribune of the plebeians (an important political post that allowed him to veto anything the senate put forward). When Ptolemy Auletes came to Rome to ask for support in getting his kingdom back, Pompey supported him; Cato and many others did not.

Pompey turned to his supporters, Crassus and the 'greatest Roman of them all', Julius Caesar. This was the first triumvirate, known to Romans then in the less positive term 'the three-headed monster'.

Cleopatra was ten; her brother Ptolemy, six. Their father, the Dionysian Piper, was in exile, forking out huge sums to buy Roman support for his return to Egypt. In the play of history, the last act of the Ptolemaic tragedy was about to be played out. And the Roman Republic would die with Cleopatra.

BOOK FOUR: CAESAR

9

THE THREE-HEADED MONSTER

ROME, 60

Gaius Julius Caesar was an immensely complex man and we need to understand him because he is the pivot between the worlds of Rome and of Cleopatra. Those worlds collided in the summer of 48 when Caesar was a war-weary veteran of fifty-two, Cleopatra a young – and exiled – queen of twenty-one. Shakespeare and countless others have reduced their relationship to a love match – a powerful celebrity figure with his much younger trophy wife – but that is to ignore complex politics and does justice to neither of them.

The Caesarii were a very old Roman family that claimed descent from the Trojan prince Aeneas who, according to one tradition, had founded Rome. The meaning of the name is obscure but – and this is a rich irony bearing in mind Julius Caesar's obsession with his lack of hair – is possibly

Oscan[31] for 'curly'. The man who would write himself into history for the next 1,000 years and beyond was born in 100, making him six years younger than Pompey, who would become first an ally and finally, a deadly rival.

In the Marius–Sulla civil war, which did so much to weaken the Republic, Caesar sided with Marius to whom he was related by marriage. The handsome young dandy, with his huge dark eyes and his habit of wearing his belt loose, was married to Cornelia, Cinna's daughter, and was given the title of *flamen dialis*, an ancient priestly order of Jupiter, which was obscure to the point of meaninglessness. On Sulla's return in 80, Caesar found himself out of a post, ordered to divorce his wife and on the run. Caught and sentenced to death, Caesar was allowed to live because of his aristocratic connections. Sulla always had his doubts about this decision – 'You are going to find many Mariuses in that boy.'[32]

The following year, Caesar began his military career on the staff of Marcus Minucius Thermus in Asia, winning a civic crown at Mitylene for saving a man's life. It was on this campaign that Caesar may have had a homosexual fling with Nicomedes, the king of Bithynia, although such charges were later levelled against his supporter Mark Antony, too. Homosexual relationships were associated by the Romans with Greek decadence, but in reality there seems to have been an ambivalence in Caesar's day that partially tolerated it. When Caesar returned to Rome in 78 the great orator and statesman Marcus Tullius Cicero quipped, 'We all know what he [Nicomedes] gave – and what you gave him.'[33] Certainly, Caesar's legions in Gaul in the years ahead sang marching songs that were very open about their commander's sexuality and it is impossible to believe he didn't hear the banter himself:

> Gaul was brought to shame by Caesar; by King Nicomedes, he.
> Here comes Caesar, wreathed in triumph for his Gallic victory!
> Nicomedes wears no laurels – though the greatest of the three.
> Here we bring our bald whoremonger; Romans, lock your
>   wives away!
> All the bags of gold you lent him, his Gallic tarts received
>   as pay.[34]

Even allowing for the ribald over-simplification, there is no disguising the fact that war, an exaggerated sex-drive and money were all very important to Caesar.

The death of Sulla opened the way for the beginnings of a political career and Caesar attempted to prosecute the governor of Cilicia, Gnaeus Cornelius Dolabella, on charges of corruption. He failed, but impressed all Rome – even the unimpressible Cicero – by his rhetoric. It was that which he went to study in Rhodes under one of the finest rhetoricians of his day, Apollonius Molon, but even here, adventure and excitement could not leave Caesar alone. Captured by the ever-menacing Cilician pirates, the future would-be emperor had to be ransomed for fifty talents. Not one to forgive or forget, Caesar raised a fleet, tracked his captors down and crucified them at Pergamon.

From 73 onwards, Caesar's career accelerated. Soon to be known for his astonishing speed on campaign, he was no slouch in politics either. First he returned to his priestly role, as augur, and used the death of his wife Cornelia and that of his aunt Julia the following year to make a public declaration of the glory of Marius' line, from whom Julia was descended. In an age when political alliances were cemented by marriage, the widower took Pompeia, Sulla's granddaughter, as his new wife. He was elected military tribune in 70, *quaestor* in 69 and *aedile* in 65. So when

Cleopatra was toddling around the marbled passageways of the royal palace in Alexandria, the man who would become her lover, protector and the father of her first child was already at the top of his political game.

Tom Holland reminds us that Romans hated being dependent on anyone[35] but in reality no one could go it totally alone in a power system as complex as republican Rome. Caesar allied himself with Marcus Licinius Crassus because he was the richest man in Rome and he almost certainly bank-rolled Caesar's campaign for the aedileship. In company with just about every other *aedile*, Caesar spent a fortune on building programmes, including restoring Marius' smashed triumphal arches on the Capitol and, of course, on the games, a move guaranteed to endear him to Romans of all classes.

Such was the size of Caesar's ego – it easily matched those of Crassus and Pompey – that he stood for the post of *Pontifex Maximus* in 63. Because this was regarded as the pinnacle of a career, which was usually given to middle-aged men who had already been censors and consuls, it was virtually earmarked for Quintus Lutatius Catulus who had been censor with Crassus two years earlier. It seemed the height of folly to a traditionalist people like the Romans that this johnny-come-lately should get the job ahead of wiser and more experienced men.

It was impossible by now for Caesar to keep out of the tangled web of Roman power-politics. Some men would have retired to their country estates, grown vines and disciplined slaves in the latifundia. But Caesar was not 'some men'. He unwisely became involved in the conspiracy of Lucius Sergius Catalina, a dangerously unstable member of an ancient family in decline. Unable to afford the massive bribes necessary to become consul, Catalina drifted ever further into the revolutionary camp, demanding that laws be passed to wipe out debt (he himself owed a fortune) and was fought every step of the way by Cicero in the senate.

The great orator was in his finest hour, but the accusations he flung at Cataline proved to be an epitaph for the Republic itself.

> In [Cataline's] bands are all the gamblers and adulterers, all the unclean and shameless citizenry. His witty, delicate boys have learned not only to love and be loved, but to use a dagger and to administer poison. If they are not driven out; if they don't die ... then I warn you, the school of Cataline will take root in our republic.[36]

Unfortunately for Rome, the school of Cataline was also the school of Publius Clodius Pulcher, and of Pompey and Caesar. Where the last two could and would use their loyal legions to attack each other, and to cow Rome into submission to them, Clodius used the mob to the same effect. Throughout the 50s, street fighting between factions was commonplace, with elections, speeches and even trials ending in mayhem with blood and cracked heads. Cicero was kicked out of the senate and of Rome; Clodius supervised first the ransacking then the physical demolition of his town house. On another occasion, Pompey had to barricade himself in to avoid an Alexandrian-style tearing apart by the mob.

Caesar himself escaped the worst of this. *Praetor* in 62, he was suspended from office for recommending that Metellus Caecilius Nepos' idea be accepted by the senate of giving Pompey a field command against Cataline who at one point joined his legions outside Rome and simply declared himself consul, thereby wiping out at a stroke the whole *raison d'être* of the Republic.

In this tumultuous period, Caesar divorced Pompeia on the wildly improbable grounds of suspicion of adultery (but in reality because her family could help him climb no higher), famously claiming that she must be 'above suspicion'.

The *propraetor* post gave Caesar an army command in Hispania Ulterior (Western Spain) and he quickly developed the strategies for which he was famous. He harassed and bullied even friendly tribes into making war and then beat them, consolidating Rome's power over the whole peninsula. He helped himself to large amounts of loot and wiped out his own debts that way, returning to Rome for a triumph and every chance of being consul. Here, however, he was blocked by envious senators spearheaded by Marcus Porcius Cato (the Younger) who was Tribune of the Plebs that year and hated everything the brash general stood for. The mob might see every Caesarean victory as a triumph for Rome and the inevitable march of civilization and progress, but to at least half the senate the man was a war criminal. Caesar was denied his triumph (no general at the head of his army could enter Rome without the senate's permission) and he was given instead command of legions in Italy on the grounds that since the revolt of Spartacus there were still bands of marauding slaves all over the place. This was virtually a policeman's job and Caesar wanted none of it. Persuading the old rivals Pompey and Crassus to work together must have taken all his ingenuity, but it worked and the three of them were, by 59, the 'three-headed monster' of the triumvirate. Crassus was the richest man in Rome; Pompey and Caesar between them had cornered the market in military prowess. They were unstoppable, especially by Caesar's co-consul, Cicero's stooge Marcus Calpurnius Bibulus.

Caesar got what he wanted – land reforms for his veterans and a command in Gaul that would turn him into a legend. Pompey got his eastern campaign ratified by the senate after years of wrangling. Crassus lined his purse even more and got command of an army against the Parthians, which would kill him. Bibulus, outmanoeuvred at every turn, retired to private life and took to watching the stars for portents. After that, he always spoke of the consulship of 'Julius and Caesar'. Increasingly, Pompey and Crassus were beginning to think the same thing.

As far as Egypt was concerned, the only Roman of the triumvirate who truly mattered was Pompey. When the three had joined forces in 60, Ptolemy Auletes appealed to the man's ego – and his love of cash – by offering him and Caesar (the Piper was presumably hedging his bets) 6,000 silver talents, half his annual revenue, to be recognized as Egypt's rightful king. Five years earlier Crassus had proposed in the senate that Rome annex Egypt as she had done with so many previously independent territories. That was rejected, as was the suggestion by the tribune Publius Servilius Rullus that Romans had a right to Egyptian land since the Republic had been named the heirs of Ptolemy VIII. But the hieroglyphs were on the wall as far as Egyptian independence was concerned and Auletes gave Pompey a gold crown for the services he rendered fighting alongside Egyptian troops in Palestine. Auletes was now in the hopeless financial 'catch-22' of having to borrow from Roman moneylenders to pay Roman politicians to stay out of Egypt. Chief among the moneylenders was Gaius

Rabirius Postumus and his work was successful enough in the short term; Auletes became officially *amicus et socinus populi Romani*, friend and ally of the Roman people. This was not empty rhetoric, but a legal contract in which Auletes held on to his throne as long as the money rolled in. How he was supposed to screw yet more money in taxation from his oppressed people at a time of Nile flooding, poor harvests and strikes was his problem.

This ignominious grovelling was in stark contrast to Auletes' brother Ptolemy, whose Cyprus was seized by Rome in 58. The excuse, which may have been justified, was that Ptolemy was aiding Cilician pirates against Rome. He was offered the role of high priest but, unable to bear the demotion from king, committed suicide instead.

Ironically, it was this failure of Auletes to help his brother that led to the Alexandrian coup against him and his replacement by his eldest daughter Berenice IV who called her aunt Cleopatra V (Auletes' sister and ex-wife) out of exile to rule with her. It was now that Auletes and his second daughter, our Cleopatra, began the wanderings we looked at in Chapter 5. In Rhodes, the vagabond king had his humiliating meeting with Marcus Porcius Cato sitting on the toilet before faring rather better in Athens and finally arriving in Italy.

The eleven-year-old Cleopatra's first visit to Rome took place in less than auspicious circumstances. Pompey, with his Alexander the Great hairstyle and pushy swagger, gave the pair and their small entourage his villa in the Alba Hills, south of Rome, but it hardly equated with the royal palace in Alexandria. The royal pair may or may not have been aware that the worship of foreign gods had been banned only six months before – an example of the increasing arrogance of the Roman establishment – but popular outcry had led to something of a U-turn and the new temple of Isis on Monte Ginesto may have been a familiar place for them to visit.

Knowing that Auletes was sucking up to the Romans, Berenice and Cleopatra Tryphaena sent a delegation to the senate to lobby against him. Auletes outmanoeuvred them with a combination of threats and bribery. It was at this juncture that the over-mighty Julius Caesar tried to get himself elected as governor of Egypt, undermining both Auletes and Pompey. He too failed and was, perhaps to keep him quiet and out of the way, given a command in Gaul, where he started as he meant to go on by provoking a war with the generally amicable Helvetii and smashing them in the process.

We have already seen that the death of Cleopatra Tryphaena threw Berenice into a panic. Her desperate search for a new co-ruler only produced the salt-fish seller who she had strangled after a week of marriage. His replacement, in the dog-eat-dog world of the Ptolemies, was Archelaos, the son of a general of Mithridates VI of Pontus who bribed the Roman governor of Syria, Aulus Gabinius, to keep out of it. But Pompey had other ideas. If Caesar had failed to get Egypt, he would not. He paid Gabinius 10,000 talents to reinstate Auletes – the man would then owe him the greatest of favours.

The triumphal entry of Auletes and the fourteen-year-old Cleopatra into Alexandria was something of a watershed. The very presence of Roman troops – Mark Antony commanded Gabinius' cavalry – spoke volumes as to who really ruled Egypt. It was now that Auletes, spiteful to the last, had his own daughter Berenice executed, and only Antony's personal intervention prevented a wholesale

Ptolemaic bloodbath. Antony's troops, mostly Gauls and Germans, stayed on in the city as a peace-keeping force, although it was not clear who was in more danger – the Alexandrians from Ptolemy or vice versa.

While Caesar was making a name for himself subduing Gaul and even invading the land at the very edge of civilization – Britannia – young Cleopatra continued her education before taking her rightful place alongside her father as co-ruler. The moneylender Rabirius accepted Auletes' offer to make him finance minister as part of the repayment, but he became so unpopular as a harsh tax collector that he had to be given a permanent bodyguard of Gauls. He ran back to Rome along with the increasingly suspect Gabinius and both men were accused of un-Roman behaviour by wearing Greek clothes! Cicero witheringly described Gabinius as a 'thieving effeminate ballet boy in curlers'.[37]

Caesar's war in Gaul is seen today as the work of a master strategist and tactician, which it was. It is also invaluable to historians as a description of the Roman war machine at work. But above all it is a piece of propaganda, and his contemporaries saw it in the simplest of terms – Caesar was lining his purse and turning himself into a hero, probably to outdo Pompey. A faction in Rome headed by Gaius Domitius Ahenobarbus planned to recall Caesar and prosecute him for alleged war crimes. Certainly the loss of life among the Gallic population was horrendous and even in an age when life was cheap there were those who felt he had much to answer for.

Even though the triumvirs met at Lucca in northern Italy and effectively renewed Caesar's Gallic contract, the very absence of the general from the hub of things lost him impetus. Crassus, too, was losing his grip. Perhaps he always intended to hide in the shadows as a string-puller, waiting for his moment, but if so, it never came. Pompey was winning laurels in the east against the Cilician pirates; Caesar was carving up Gaul. Crassus had only one clear victory to his name and although Spartacus was possibly more of a general than anyone Pompey or Caesar faced, his was still an army of slaves and there was no glory in that. Because of that, Crassus, having served as co-consul with Pompey for a second time, insisted on a five-year command in the east.

It was perhaps unfortunate for him that his enemies were the skilled and resourceful Parthians whose cataphracts (heavy cavalry) could smash through Roman infantry, even when that infantry were the formidable legions. At Carrhae (Haran in modern Turkey) in 53 Crassus was stopped in his tracks and his son Publius was killed. In 'peace talks' the next day Crassus was struck down as he tried to mount his horse. His head and hand were hacked off and sent to Armenia. The head of the richest man in Rome would make one last appearance. In the celebrations after Carrhae, a Greek play was staged for the Parthian generals. During it, an actor dressed as a maenad, a devotee of Dionysus so loved by Auletes and so detested by Rome, threw the head in the air and it was kicked from player to player in the sand.

In the previous year, the last family link between the two remaining triumvirs was broken. Pompey's fourth wife was Julia Caesar, the daughter of the conqueror of Gaul. There is little doubt that Pompey genuinely loved her, but she died in childbirth and an ambitious, successful Roman was obliged to remarry. His choice was typically quirky and political. Cornelia was the daughter of Caecilius Metellus Scipio and the widow of the Publius Crassus killed at

Carrhae. She was sophisticated and beautiful, but more importantly linked to the family of the Scipio who had defeated Hannibal and destroyed Carthage. It was like marrying into the Kennedy family in late-twentieth-century America. The marriage – Pompey's fifth – saw him move out of Caesar's camp for ever. And Pompey didn't put a foot wrong. He staged the most lavish games Rome had ever seen in September 55, with elephants, tigers, rhinoceros, leopards, wolves and even a cephos, an Ethiopian animal with the feet of a man that was probably a baboon, all of them urged to fight each other and end their days screaming in agony on the spearheads and tridents of the *bestiarii*, the animal gladiators.

There is no doubt that Pompey regarded himself as the most powerful man in Rome. He had served twice as consul and was still governor of Spain with a formidable military reputation, yet in the elections that followed the games, his bid to bribe the electorate with bread and circuses failed. Domitius Ahenobarbus was consul for 54 and Cato was *praetor*. Increasingly, Cato set himself up as the man of the Republic, creaking though it obviously was. He had no armies at his back, unlike both Pompey and Caesar. He had no money, unlike the recently deceased Crassus, to bribe men to vote for him. He just stood for honesty and that which was most dear to all Romans, tradition.

But it all turned to ashes. By 53–52 charges of corruption were being levelled at Ahenobarbus and his fellow consul Appius Claudius Pulcher (the Handsome) and street fighting broke out between Cato's thug Titus Annius Milo and Clodius, the youngest of Appius Claudius' sons. Using street gangs and gladiators from the training schools, both men indulged in open warfare in which nobody's life was safe. Things came to a head on the night of 18 January 52 when Milo and Clodius met face to face. In the scuffle that followed, Clodius was hit in the shoulder with a javelin and he was carried, bleeding profusely, to a tavern along the Appian Way, Milo's men in hot pursuit. They dragged him outside and hacked him to death.

It was in the nature of things that matters could not rest there. Clodius was ever a man of the people – even the spelling of his name reflected the plebs' pronunciation of Claudius – and the mob went on the rampage in revenge, almost exactly as they would with the murder of Caesar twelve years later. They smashed their way into the senate house the next day and built a pyre for Clodius from the shattered furniture. The blaze destroyed the entire building and the law courts next door. The superstitious Romans got the point – the Republic was a burned-out husk.

In desperation the senate turned to Pompey. They granted him the consulship as long as he restored law and order. This was halfway to dictatorship and it had been achieved as far as Pompey was concerned without bloodshed. Now he unleashed his legions, beating the street gangs at their own game. Milo was put on trial for the murder of Clodius and even the renowned orator Cicero, charged with defending him, was overawed by the unthinkable – a ring of shields around the Forum. Milo was found guilty and got off lightly by being allowed to sail into exile in Marseille, in Caesar's Gaul.

Ptolemy the Piper died on 7 March 51 during a partial solar eclipse, the gods, as always, marking the coming and the going of a demi-god. There is debate how old he was, but he was probably sixty, and after a turbulent life – and unlike most of the Ptolemies – his death was due to natural causes. His will, which had been ratified by the Roman senate, when they weren't screaming at each other, stipulated that Cleopatra Thea Philopator, the father-loving goddess, should rule jointly with her ten-year-old brother Ptolemy XIII. It is at least likely that Cleopatra kept the news of the old king's death secret except to her innermost circle for as long as she could. It is difficult to be sure but there seems to have been no love lost between the siblings and when a petulant little boy happens to be co-ruler of a great country and heir of a great dynasty, the petty rivalries of the nursery assume gigantic and horrific proportions. Ptolemy's advisers might have staged a coup to remove Cleopatra, even though she was eighteen and had almost certainly been ruling alongside her father for the last eighteen months. It was not until 30 June that Rome heard of Auletes' death, by which time the king had been embalmed in the Egyptian tradition with its ten-week ritual of binding, amulet-placing and incense.

The will of Auletes was copied – one version was placed on the stone shelves of the great library in Alexandria; the other went to Pompey's villa near Rome. Ominously for the last of the Ptolemies, the Roman people were declared guardians and protectors of the land of Egypt.

Nobody except Cleopatra missed Auletes. Latterly he had given lavish banquets paid for by taxing the Egyptian people, drank himself into a stupor and had indiscriminate sex with male and female teenagers. Even so, Cleopatra and her brother inherited a throne protected by the greatest military power in the world and the priesthood backed them both as pharaohs in a tradition that was centuries old.

10

CROSSING THE RIVERS

THE RUBICON, 49

One of Cleopatra's first acts as queen was to honour the Buchis bull. A funerary stela now in the Carlsberg Glyptotek museum in Copenhagen reads:

> The queen, the lady of the Two Lands, the Goddess Philopator, rowed [the bull] in the boat of Amun, together with the other boats of the king, all the inhabitants of Thebes and Hermonthis and priests being with [them].[38]

This was standard practice; in fact, the exact form of words can be found in earlier carved records. What it proves is that Egypt welcomed the new queen with open arms and there is a smooth sense of continuity from Auletes. The Buchis bull belonged to the complex religious rites we saw in Book One, an animal chosen because it was identified with Osiris, the fertility-god and god of the Underworld; with Montu, the warrior-god, and with the sun-god Ra. Montu was identified by the Alexandrian Greeks as Apollo because of his links with the sun. His later effigies, those from Cleopatra's reign, show him as a bull-headed man in the Minotaur tradition, with two tall plumes fixed to his horns. He carried the *khepesh*, a curved sword, and in many bas-reliefs from the New Kingdom is shown offering the weapon to pharaoh to enable the man to defeat his enemies. As we have seen, the Egyptians brought offerings to the animal, its horns bedecked with garlands and it could predict the future and cure the sick. It even changed colour every hour, and to encourage fertility, women appeared in front of it, according to a horrified Herodotus, exposing their genitals. When the bull died it was mummified and laid to rest in a ceremony called the *Bucheion* in Greek at Hermonthis on the Nile, south of Thebes.

It may seem strange that all modern accounts of Cleopatra make great play of this tradition, but it is a reminder of the huge importance of religion in the ancient world and of tradition. Elizabeth II of England was crowned in Westminster Abbey in AD 1952 and went through essentially the same coronation ceremony that her ancestors had for 1,000 years.

Many historians, too, make great play of the fact that Cleopatra's reign marks the end of the Ptolemies and that what we are looking at is a dynasty in decline. There is some comparison with the reign of Nicholas II in Russia in the early twentieth century. His family, the Romanovs, had, like the Ptolemies, ruled their country for three centuries. There was also an air of 'foreignness' about them – Nicholas was Russian but his wife was not and the pair wrote letters and diary entries in English. Nicholas Romanov was the richest man in the world until AD 1917, as was Cleopatra before 31. What destroyed Nicholas was his inability to cope with demands for change from within. What destroyed Cleopatra was Rome. But there was nothing inevitable about either case.

The immediate problem for Cleopatra in 51 was her brother Ptolemy XIII. They may have married soon after Auletes' death, although there is no record of it and if it happened it could only have been to prevent any sense of rivalry between 'her' court and 'his'. Then, as now, one of the first priorities of a monarch was to provide an heir so that the dynasty can continue. At eighteen, Cleopatra was of eminently marriageable age; Ptolemy, of course, was still too young. It may have been simply a matter of his age or it may have been a conscious ploy on her part, but until 49 Ptolemy is invisible. In a stela from the Faiyum Delta, she appears as a man, in the typical straight-legged profile of Egyptian pharaohs, wearing the crown of the two lands, apparently proclaiming her as sole ruler. It is only the inscription that makes it clear who this is. Experts are divided over the importance of this evidence. Is it a deliberate statement by Cleopatra, doing a man's job despite her female body (and in this sense she echoes the female pharaoh Hatsheput in the New Kingdom) or was this simply a piece of artwork made for Auletes which had a new inscription added?

Cleopatra intended to impress from day one, whether it be her own Alexandrians, the people of Upper Egypt, toiling away in the flood plain of the Nile, or the Romans edging ever nearer to her mouth-wateringly rich kingdom. And dress was all important. In Alexandria she wore her (possibly auburn) hair in a melon bun with a simple gold diadem and an expensive but not over-gaudy dress of Greek design. In this attire she would have found favour even with the Roman matrons surrounding Pompey and Caesar who were starchy in the extreme. When she took the title Neos Dionysus (the New Dionysus) from her father, underlying her closeness to him and her deep religiosity, Cleopatra wore white under a striking black robe as worn by the priesthood. For the Egyptians she went completely over the top with the help of her wardrobe mistress, Charmion. She wore the tight-fitting sheath dress (which, although sexy and elegant must have been very difficult to walk in) and a colourful splash of precious stones and vulture feathers. It was a conscious effort to appear at one with the gods and the ancient pharaohs. As the goddess Isis (which the Egyptians still called Aset during Cleopatra's reign), she appeared in her full royal regalia with the red and white crowns of Lower and Upper Egypt with the rearing cobra (*uraeus*) in gold on her forehead.

In an age before widespread literacy and instant telecommunication, it was important that Cleopatra show herself to her people as often as possible. In a sense that was made easy by the geography of Egypt. It *was* the Nile and the dedication of the Buchis bull on 22 March 52 was part of a river journey designed to impress and reassure Egyptians of all classes.

Built into this river journey – and the later one she made with Caesar – was the physical existence and symbolic *idea* of her barge. There is no clear contemporary description of it. Shakespeare's famous image of gold burning on water comes from Plutarch who was writing two centuries after Cleopatra, but it is entirely in keeping with the floating palace of the queen. It may have been 300 feet long with a cypress wood hull decorated with ivory, gold and silver. It had awnings and carved statues on the deck, shrines to the gods like Isis and Dionysus, and perhaps even a library, a gymnasium, a lecture hall and an aquarium. It was the setting for her seduction of Mark Antony and may even, in modified form, have taken part in the naval battle of Actium. Smaller boats clustered around it, bearing priests and local officials, at every step of the way.

We know that she attended the ceremony of the Apis bull at Memphis, Egypt's ancient capital, in 49 and paid 412 silver coins, as well as providing food for the animal's extensive priesthood. She may have been overdoing her relationship with her Egyptian subjects at the expense of the Alexandrians and that could have been a mistake due to her youth. There had been revolts from time to time along the Nile, against taxation and bad harvests, but the clear and present danger came from the multicultural city in Cleopatra's own backyard. Alexandria's population had a reputation for unrest and thought little, as we have seen, of dragging unpopular rulers to the Gymnasion for a good slaughtering. By the autumn of 50, it was clear that brother Ptolemy felt he had been kept in the shadows long enough. He was still only twelve but his three principal advisers – Potheinos, his nurse; Theodotus, his tutor, and Achillas, his general – were itching to usurp Cleopatra and began by grabbing the all-important grain supplies to Alexandria. Decrees were now issued in the joint names of Ptolemy XIII and Cleopatra and the order of the names was lost on no one. This was 'Year One' for him and Cleopatra must have realized that her resources were far from limitless. Auletes had died broke, having paid so much blood money to Rome, and the floods along the Nile in 51–50 had led to poor harvests and harsh taxation. This probably explains Cleopatra's open and ostentatious wooing of the priests.

Keep the priests happy and, by and large, the people were happy too. Twelve hundred miles away, things weren't going too well for Rome either.

In the summer of 52 news reached Rome that Caesar had won a crushing victory at Alesia in Gaul. Plutarch estimated that the general 'fought pitched battles at various times with three million men, of whom he destroyed one million in the actual fighting and took another million prisoners'.[39] The Romans were notorious liars when it came to propaganda figures, but there is no doubt that Alesia was the high or low point (depending on our point of view) of slaughter that was both unnecessary and deliberately provoked by Caesar. His opponents in the senate (and they were many) mostly saw this as yet another example of the blood-craze of a warmonger. His supporters, however, wanted him to return to a triumph (for which the Plebs cheered heartily) and to become consul again. If that should happen, with the heaven-storming legions at his back, nothing could stop him.

Cato, as usual, stood firmly behind the increasingly obsolete standards of republicanism. So did Cicero. Caesar spent some of his loot money bribing senators back home. 'By now,' wrote Petronius years later under the emperor Nero, 'the conquering Roman had the whole world in his hand, the sea, the land, the course of the stars. But still he wanted more.'[40] The generic 'conquering Roman' could apply equally to Caesar and to Pompey and at first, when Pompey was called upon to take his former friend and son-in-law down a peg or two, he took to his bed with a convenient illness. But the clash was coming – of that there was no doubt.

In December 50 the consul Gaius Marcellus, with a large crowd of senators and the usual morbidly curious mob, went to see Pompey in his villa in the Alban Hills. Gaius Marcellus told him to march against Caesar, and Pompey accepted. On behalf of Caesar, the Tribune of the Plebs, Mark Antony, read out the general's letter to the senate. It spoke of peace, harmony and the good of Rome but few people were listening and Metellus Scipio demanded that Caesar give up his legions or be declared an outlaw. Only two senators opposed the bill and although Antony vetoed it, the moment had come.

Martial law was declared on 7 January 49 with Pompey's legions from Capua patrolling the streets. Antony and the two loyal senators fled, apparently disguised as slaves, to Ravenna where Caesar was camped with the 13th Legion. With the kind of panache that the Duke of Wellington exhibited at the Duchess of Richmond's ball shortly before Waterloo in AD 1815, Caesar had a bath and went to a banquet before riding to join his troops on the banks of the Rubicon, an unimportant little stream swollen by the winter rains, in the north of Italy.

We do not know exactly when or how Ptolemy XIII's coup against his sister took place. It is likely to have been in the spring of 49 and by the summer Ptolemy was regarded as Egypt's sole ruler. The eunuch nurse Potheinos gave himself the title of minister of finance and the fickle Alexandrians seemed happy with that for the time being.

Cleopatra was on the run, but only from Alexandria. Her assiduous courtship of Upper Egypt now paid off. She reached Thebes and crossed the desert to the Red Sea. With her was a sizeable army under the highly efficient general Callimachos and she established a rival court to Ptolemy's at Askalon near Gaza. Speaking fluent Aramaic and Hebrew as she did, she was able to talk politics directly to local officials without the services of an interpreter. Even allowing for the fact that the area had long been loyal to the Ptolemies, the men who flocked to her now were in effect being asked to take sides in a civil war in which they had no direct interest and to choose between siblings of the same house. In getting an army together at all, Cleopatra was achieving the impossible and she coolly had coins struck at Askalon. Her portrait on these shows the twenty-year-old as a younger, only slightly female version of her father, with large eyes, a hooked nose and firm, resolute mouth. She would need all her resolution in the months ahead.

With hindsight, Pompey made a wrong call to abandon Rome. The Rubicon, minor irritant as it was geographically to an experienced army used to handling dangerous river-crossings, was the sacred boundary between Gaul and Roman Italy. It was also a line in the sand. Technically, Caesar's advancing legions could have halted at any time, but the crossing of the Rubicon was a symbolic act, a declaration of war, and it duly entered the Latin and later the English language as a point from which there could be no going back.

Caesar trotted south with the 13th at his back, marching in double time, leaving his remaining four legions to catch up when they could. His speed wrong-footed Pompey who effectively told Rome it was on its own and marched his legions south. Tom Holland says, 'Pompey, of course, could argue that there were sound military reasons for the surrender of the capital – and so there were',[41] but it is difficult to think of any. Rome could be taken militarily by any army with ballistae (missiles) to smash its walls but the Gauls and even the great Hannibal had both failed years before and it would be four centuries before Alaric the Visigoth sacked the place. Much more importantly, Rome was *the* symbol of the Republic – leave it in an enemy's hands, even a Roman enemy, and there would be no Republic. And there was a fifty-fifty chance that Caesar's legions, loyal to him though they were, might refuse to march on their own homes.

Terrified citizens, if they were rich enough, fled south. Only a tiny handful of senators remained, leaving the city defenceless, not only against Caesar, but against the mob who must have realized that the rule of law had collapsed. Domitius Ahenobarbus tried to rally troops against Caesar at Corfinium, but his inexperienced troops ran at the sight of Caesar's grim *calligae*[42] and Ahenobarbus was brought before Caesar. The rebel was spared, as was the town; a stroke of genius from Caesar because all the towns in Italy, including Rome itself, knew there would be no destruction, no crucifixions, if they surrendered to him.

Pompey reached Brundisium, the port in the south-east, and commandeered any sailing boat he could to get his men off the peninsula, bound for Greece. The fast-marching Caesar caught him there and bombarded his ramparts with slingshots and heavy artillery. Even so, he could not close the harbour and Pompey and his entire command slipped away into the night. With various senators with him and others scattered as far away from Rome as they felt safe, the defender of the Republic (as he billed himself now) holed up in Thessalonica to await events. He invited various client kings to his side. The Galatians arrived under Deiotarus, the Cappadocians under Ariobarzanes, the Commagenians led by Antiochus. He couldn't know it yet, but with these auxiliaries, his army outnumbered Caesar's two to one.

Pompey may have had a plan to starve Rome out by cutting off food supplies from the provinces, but if so, it was not feasible. He had loyal legions in Spain, so effectively he controlled east and west but in the days of slow and limited communication, coordinating those disparate troops to strangle Caesar in the centre was never likely to work.

When Caesar reached Rome, few people turned up to hear his public proclamations. He was not greeted as a conquering hero and the tribune Caecilius Metellus tried to stop him from entering the treasury in the town's temple of Saturn. Faced with death, Metellus backed down, but now there could be no pretence. Caesar had crossed the Rubicon and the Tiber. He had brought troops into the sacred city, had occupied the heart of Rome itself and had grabbed its valuables. He was a dictator in all but name.

Leaving the cavalry commander Marcus Lepidus to govern the city in his absence, Caesar sailed for Spain in the summer of 49 and smashed Pompey's three legions there before Pompey knew what was happening. With Caesar in Spain, Pompey could have landed in Italy and probably retaken the city (Lepidus would have been no threat) but he seems to have been struck by a deadly lethargy and no one in military history moved as fast as Caesar.

Elsewhere, his supporters fared less well. Gaius Scribonius Curio, once anti-Caesar but now won over to his side by cash, was one of the two senators who had voted against both Caesar and Pompey retaining their commands. He occupied Sicily for Caesar and crossed to Africa. Here he faced Pompey's general Publius Attius Varus and King Juba of Numidia. His legions were wiped out in the Bagrades Valley and he died with them. Marcus Caelius Rufus was no safer in Rome itself. He tried to raise the people on behalf of

Pompey, having had his legislative ideas turned down by the senate, and was killed in the violence that followed.

Early in 48, with storms battering the Adriatic, Caesar eluded Pompey's numerically superior fleet and reached Greece. Here, in a grim winter, his troops were in danger of starving and the *calligae* were forced to make bread from grass. There were alarms and excursions, with the odd head-on clash, but Pompey was not anxious to meet Caesar in the field and in terms of their reputation, Caesar probably had the upper hand. 'This man', he had come to realize, 'does not know how to win wars.'[43]

At Dyrrachium (in today's Albania) in July, a siege stalemate ended in Caesar getting a bloody nose. Again, we cannot rely on the numbers involved, but Caesar's casu alties are said to have been 1,000, Pompey's far fewer. Caesar withdrew into northern Greece and Pompey should have turned the retreat into a rout or taken this second opportunity to sail for Rome. He did neither, but faced Caesar again at Pharsalus on 9 August.

Caesar may have had 22,000 infantry, but Pompey had 45,000 and his cavalry outnumbered Caesar's by seven to one. It was this horsed advantage that Pompey planned to capitalize on, especially as the field at Pharsalus was broad and flat, excellent cavalry country. We have to remember that nearly half of Pompey's troops, perhaps more, were auxiliaries, not trained in the Roman style and certainly lacking Caesar's legions' recent gruelling experience in Gaul. Pompey's second in command, Titus Labienus, attacked with his cavalry on his left flank, intending to demoralize Caesar's flimsy cavalry force and then hit the centre from the flank. Caesar, of course, had anticipated this and placed six cohorts in the triple-acies (three-line) formation behind his cavalry. As predicted, the dictator's horsemen broke in the face of a headlong charge, but Caesar's hidden infantry advanced, using their javelins as spears, and Pompey's cavalry broke up, allowing Caesar to hit his centre in exactly the same way that his enemy had planned.

Quickly stripping a cohort from the rear line of each legion, Caesar effectively created a fourth line which crashed forward through the front lines to shatter Pompey's centre. We have noted already the dubious casualty figures written for posterity, often by much later writers; Caesar claimed to have only 200 casualties as opposed to Pompey's 15,000. A further 24,000 were captured and no less than nine legionary eagles were taken. Even if the figures themselves were exaggerated, the results were self-evident. Pompey had lost and his army was destroyed. His wife, Cornelia, may have rallied her husband with a positive pep talk as various commentators contend, but he had no army left to renew the war. Or did he?

We do not know whether Pompey had summoned Ptolemy and Cleopatra to join him at Thessalonica. On balance it seems unlikely because Egypt was a 'friend and ally' of Rome, not technically a client kingdom, and they owed no such military obligation. At this point, of course, we have a bizarre situation. Both nations were waging civil war. Egypt may have been beholden to Rome, but which Rome: Caesar's or Pompey's? And if Pompey was asking for help, to whom did he turn – Cleopatra or Ptolemy?

The latter question is easier to answer. In September 48 the power in Alexandria was unquestionably Ptolemy and his advisers. Cleopatra was miles to the east, in a desert wilderness at the edge of the Nile delta that might just as well have been the far side of the moon. So Pompey waited with a little naval flotilla off the Pharos while his people talked to Ptolemy's. On 28 September, a fishing boat was sent out to bring Pompey to meet the boy king in person. While Ptolemy watched from a litter-borne throne on the quayside and Cornelia looked on from the ships at the harbour entrance, an extraordinary melodrama was played out. When Pompey struggled ashore in the shallows, the water presumably water-logging his cloak, one of his attendants, Septimus, who had fought under him as a centurion, plunged a dagger into the general's back. Another ex-comrade, Salvius, rammed his dagger home and the slave Philippus held his master's hand as Achillas, Ptolemy's general, hacked off the head of the great Pompey. 'He neither said nor did anything unworthy of himself,' Plutarch wrote years later, 'only groaned a little and so ended his life in the sixtieth year and only one day after his birthday.'[44]

Philippus, in floods of tears, washed the headless corpse in sea water and loaded it into a nearby fishing boat. He set fire to it in a funeral pyre on the beach, which was still burning the next day. An anonymous ex-comrade of Pompey was there at the time and Plutarch records him as saying, 'I find this happiness at last, to touch with my hands and to prepare for burial the body of the greatest Imperator that Rome has seen.'[45]

Ptolemy knew, as any cynic did, that 'dead men don't bite' but a live one was on his way in pursuit of Pompey – Gaius Julius Caesar.

The new dictator arrived three days later with perhaps 4,000 men. Typically he had not waited until his entire army had licked their wounds after Pharsalus and knew he could track down Pompey with far fewer men than he had. Ptolemy's army were massed to the east of Alexandria, since

that was the direction Cleopatra would arrive from, but the
arrival of Caesar in the harbour brought Potheinos and
Theodotus scurrying to meet him. They showed him the
head of Pompey and his signet ring with its lion and sword
motif. Caesar wept. Historians cannot decide how crocodile
these tears were. Nobody could wish the man dead more
than Caesar, but nostalgia played its part here – Pompey
had, after all, been his son-in-law and former friend. His
tears may have been of shock and disgust, confirming in
Caesar what he had probably always heard, that the
Ptolemies were a pack of ravening wolves. With his lictors
carrying their axes and bundles, the symbol of Rome's
authority, he marched to Ptolemy's palace and took it over.
The Alexandrians, predictably, rioted and there were several
deaths.

Caesar stayed. He gave the reason that winds kept his
ships penned in the harbour, but he probably intended to
milk Alexandria for all it had. He had never seen the astonishing city before and was probably genuinely overawed by
it. He visited the Pharos lighthouse, rummaged through the
scrolls in the library and paid homage at the tomb of
Alexander. He dictated his memoirs and played for time.
Then, like an old-fashioned headmaster arbitrating between
playground squabbles, he ordered Ptolemy and Cleopatra
to disband their armies and appear before him – two rulers
by divine right on the carpet of a warlord.

11

THE LADY OF THE TWO LANDS

ALEXANDRIA, 48

Carpets play a significant role in the folklore of the Middle East and legend has it that this is how Caesar and Cleopatra met. Like a malevolent spider at the centre of his web, the eunuch Potheinos tried to manipulate both sides for his own ends. He let it be known that Caesar's men were dining off the Ptolemies' silver when in fact they were eating from wooden trenchers and the grain they were fed was rotten. In the desert to the east, Cleopatra now considered the time was right to get her throne back. Ptolemy appeared to have all the cards – he was in possession of Alexandria whose inhabitants by and large backed him as their rightful king. He also had the Gabinian troops as a formidable bodyguard and perhaps he could persuade the legendary Caesar to add his 4,000, as well as his huge military expertise, to his cause.

For his part, Caesar was suspicious of the set-up in Alexandria. Rioting townspeople didn't bother him – he was a Roman, after all – but the pharaoh was only fourteen and it was clear that his strings were being pulled by a trio of self-serving degenerates – a eunuch, a teacher and a mercenary. And they had all connived to murder Pompey.

Neither Ptolemy nor his sister had disbanded their armies as Caesar had ordered, but Cleopatra knew she had to reach the general somehow and Ptolemy would not give her safe conduct through his lines. So she sailed in a fishing boat with her faithful attendant Apollodorus up the Nile into Alexandria and he carried her ashore. Historians have argued about this bizarre entrance for centuries. The queen of Egypt wrapped in a carpet only really fits in a *Carry On* film[46] and almost certainly is not what happened. She was probably heavily veiled in the *himatia*, a Greek hood and cloak resembling the burka worn by strict Muslim women today.

There was no problem for Cleopatra to get into the royal palace; she had probably been born in the place and must have known every passageway and secret door. Apollodorus spoke fluent Latin so he could have talked his way out of trouble with either the Gabinian guards of Ptolemy or Caesar's men. Even so, it is inconceivable that Apollodorus and his disguised companion could have gained easy access to Caesar. If proof were needed, the fate of Pompey proved that assassination came easily to the Egyptians. Caesar must have known of Cleopatra's visit in advance and while he too understood the need for secrecy, he was not at all alarmed by it.

All modern commentators – and most of them are women – spend a considerable time wrestling with just how this famous meeting went. For all the striven-for gender equality of the last hundred years, they are obsessed with what she wore. Nobody asks what Caesar had on. The point is that an important weapon in Cleopatra's armoury was her sexuality. She was twenty-one, perhaps twenty-two; her sexual experience is unknown. Caesar was fifty-two, a veteran of the bedroom as he was of the battlefield. He had been married four times and was a notorious womanizer. No doubt Cleopatra had done her homework on this man and if she had heard the rumours concerning King Nicomedes, she probably assumed that they were exaggerated or at any rate her charms could win the general over.

Stacy Schiff's title of the relevant chapter in her book says it all – 'Cleopatra Captures the Old Man by Magic'.[47] She did not simply strip off and offer herself to Caesar; the seduction was far more complex – and important – than that. And it is by no means clear who seduced whom. It is easy to turn this into a Mills & Boon romance or even soft porn, but we have to remember the realpolitik of the situation. As the most powerful member of the Mediterranean's master race, Caesar could offer protection to Egypt and could win Cleopatra's throne back for her. On her part, she was queen of the Mediterranean's bread basket; if Rome controlled the Nile, the City of the Seven Hills was unstoppable.

If we deal merely in physical superficialities, we are actually looking at a living god and goddess. Caesar was leather-hard from years of campaigning, but nearly bald and a sufferer from petit mal – the 'sleeping sickness' that would sometimes cause fits. In an age when fertility was everything, he had only fathered one legitimate child – Julia – and she was dead. He had terrifying nightmares and was known to be dangerously magnanimous to defeated enemies, something of a weakness in the ancient world. Laying aside all the platitudes of commentators then and since who want to see

Cleopatra as a femme fatale, much of her charm was her bubbling personality and genuinely melodic voice. Various portraits of her show a nose too hooked, a tight, mean-looking mouth and a neck with wrinkles, even in her twenties, which suggests thyroid problems.

Was she a virgin? We have no idea. Given the Ptolemies' penchant for incest, any lover is likely to have been a family member and she did co-rule with Auletes for almost eighteen months. If the only sexual experience she had had was with her father, it might explain an instant attraction for Caesar, the classic older man of women's literature. What probably excited her was power. Caesar was a hero in the mould of Alexander himself, and all Rome – and therefore the civilized world – lay at his feet. He in turn may have been captivated by her radiance and bowled over by her courage and impudence. In smuggling herself into his presence she had carried out exactly the kind of impulsive action that he had done all his life. At home was his wife Calpurnia, who has assumed something akin to sainthood because of the dignified way she handled her husband's assassination in 44. In fact, he had already divorced her in 53 to marry Pompey's daughter and even the original marriage was merely one of political convenience. Cleopatra must have seemed an astonishing breath of fresh, if exotic and spice-laden, air after that.

Plutarch's account has Cleopatra having time to make herself beautiful between rolling out of Apollodorus' cloak/canvas sack/carpet and meeting Caesar, but this seems unlikely. Would he have been more enchanted by a dishevelled, wide-eyed girl on the run, breathlessly begging his help or a cool seductress in full make-up? Perhaps it was Plutarch's inability to explain the attraction that meant that, in his account, he hedged his bets.

The unlikely couple did not necessarily go to bed together that night but it is likely to have been soon after because all Caesar's actions for the next three months are either with Cleopatra or on her behalf. The next pressing problem was Ptolemy and his army and when the boy discovered that his big sister was not only back in *his* palace, but had pulled the linen over Caesar's eyes, he stormed out in tears, wailing to passers-by that he had been betrayed. Caesar's guards brought him back and put him under house arrest.

The victor of Pharsalus and so many other battles now had the most important of Auletes' children in his charge, one willingly, the other not. He knew perfectly well that the scheming Potheinos had the other two – seventeen-year-old Arsinoe and the boy Ptolemy XIV – and that sooner or later he would use them as trump cards. It was in Caesar's interests – and Rome's – to effect a reconciliation between Cleopatra and her nearest brother. But one thing was abundantly clear: Rome would not take a back seat in Egyptian affairs again.

Caesar had almost certainly misread the mood of the Alexandrians who had swallowed whole the propaganda of Potheinos/Ptolemy that Cleopatra was evil itself. He made a speech – for the gifted orator, no problem – from a palace balcony and did the headmasterly thing with Auletes' squabbling children in front of him. Rather than the riot act, he read them their father's will. They must rule Egypt together under Roman guardianship. Arsinoe and Ptolemy XIV should have Cyprus, the island so recently lost to Rome when Auletes' brother had swallowed poison rather than let Rome in.

Amid rumours that Potheinos was conspiring to poison Caesar (it was well known that he would eat anything), Caesar realized that Alexandria was on the point of open rebellion against him and the Roman presence. The order to assassinate

Potheinos made perfect sense given the man's ambition and dangerous nature, but to Alexandrians it was a cause for war.

Rattled, Caesar sent ambassadors to Achillas, commanding Ptolemy's army outside the city to open negotiations. The general had the men hacked down before they reached his tent. In his account, Caesar plays down the desperate nature of the Egyptian war he was now obliged to fight. His legions had not yet arrived from Greece and he was heavily outnumbered. Low on food and fresh water in the royal palace, he ordered his legionaries to dig until they found underground streams. For men used to digging trenches and building marching camps on campaign, this was bread and butter to them, but they were harried night and day by missile attacks and attempts to breach the palace walls.

And now Arsinoe escaped. After the removal of Potheinos, Caesar had all three children holed up in the palace, but Arsinoe was a Ptolemy through and through. Every bit as resourceful and calculating as Cleopatra, she was proclaimed queen in Alexandria and appeared at every opportunity alongside Achillas, now 'her' general. During the street fighting, the Egyptian fleet returned. It comprised fifty warships lent by Cleopatra to Pompey and both sides were desperate to get their hands on them. Caesar got there first, but had no time to do anything but set them alight to prevent them falling into Achillas' hands. The fire, that terrifying night, spread to the town from the harbour and destroyed part of Alexandria's fabled library. In the fierce fluttering of the flames, Caesar's little garrison fought hand to hand with Achillas' Egyptians, determined to drive the Romans out. Not to be outdone, the Alexandrians rebuilt the fleet in a matter of days, making it impossible for Caesar to escape.

The one light at the end of the tunnel for the beleaguered Romans was the in-fighting between their enemies. Arsinoe, with her tutor Ganymedes, poisoned Achillas in a coup that made no sense at all. In January 47 a delegation of towns-people came under a flag of truce to Caesar to ask him to release Ptolemy, their rightful king. Clearly, Arsinoe had plans to oust Cleopatra and by marrying her brother and ruling with him, this would have the cloak of legality. Caesar could see the point of this in his favour, too – he may have been prepared to jettison Cleopatra at this stage – in order to achieve a Roman-controlled Egypt. In a bizarre scene that looks Hollywood-inspired, the crusty old general sat down with the moody pharaoh and told it like it was. Ptolemy cried; the rumour was that Caesar did too and in the end they parted company sadly, rather as father and son. As soon as he was free, Ptolemy took command of Achillas' army, complete in golden armour, and marched to face Caesar's reinforcements, Anatolian and Syrian troops under the king of Pergamon. A further 3,000 joined this band under Antipatros, father of the Herod of Bible infamy. They took Pelusium and marched towards present-day Cairo where Ptolemy's army was caught in a classic pincer movement with Caesar's troops. The boy pharaoh went down in the Nile delta, drowning in his golden armour and his body was never found.

In the victory celebrations that followed, we see Cleopatra behaving every inch a queen. It could be argued, as the Romans did, that she only sat on the throne because of Caesar and as long as Rome let her, but what followed were the years of her greatness, leading, perhaps, to the ultimate tragedy. The couple visited the shrine of Alexander the Great and Caesar left his purple robe and rings there as votive offerings. He buried the embalmed head of Pompey in the Nemesion, a tomb near the city wall, and erected a pillar to the Jews of the city who had taken his and Cleopatra's side over the previous weeks.

A peculiar piece of politics now took place. Caesar decided, almost certainly with Cleopatra's full backing, that she should become co-ruler, if only in name, with her remaining brother, now twelve, who became Ptolemy XIV. They were formally Theoi Philopatores Philadelphia, father-loving, sibling-loving gods. Cleopatra then married Caesar, although marriage in Ptolemaic Egypt had little in the way of religious solemnity attached to it. From Caesar's point of view, he was committing bigamy, not to mention adultery, and Roman law would never see Cleopatra as anything other than his mistress. When Octavian's propaganda machine got its claws into her ten years later, she became a whore whose sexual excesses were made worse by the use of magic. This was the only way to explain what had happened to Caesar and what would later happen to Mark Antony.

Celebrations were held in Alexandria, both to mark the peace and to celebrate the restoration of the rightful rulers of Egypt. From there, the next step would be to sail and row south, down the Nile and for the same reasons that Cleopatra had undertaken it when Auletes died. This was not a honeymoon, with idyllic lovers on the Nile drinking their nights away under a romantic moon. This was Cleopatra the hard-headed politician visiting the shrines and temples of old Egypt, reconfirming her one-ness with gods and people, reminding them who she was. And if, on her arm, or a politic half step behind, was the man who bestrode the narrow world like a colossus, it only added to her power. There were, no doubt, those who saw it differently; Cleopatra ruled because Rome let her. Her gilded barge rippled the Nile because the bald whoremonger had said it should be so. And for Caesar, it possibly was a welcome holiday. The couple took to the river with a flotilla of 400 ships, including a sizeable bodyguard of Caesar's veterans. Given the situation, it is unlikely that any of them were Roman war-galleys, but they were probably the rebuilt ships of Cleopatra's fleet that Caesar had burned in the harbour during the hectic weeks of the siege.

Joann Fletcher highlights the sights that Caesar would have seen, reminding us always that Cleopatra's real purpose was to give thanks and offerings to the various temples we described in Chapter 2. Much of this would have been awe-inspiring to Caesar, a reminder that his own nation was pitifully new and rather vulgar by comparison with the antiquity of Egypt.

Aboard their floating palace, the royal couple (in Egypt, though never Rome, Caesar was viewed as a living god) were entertained by priests and local officials on both banks of the Nile. This was ruinously expensive for the host, in that Cleopatra was a guest and not expected to pick up the tab. One surviving account refers to 200 sheep and 372 suckling pigs as the meat course of a much larger banquet. Caesar must have been impressed; Egypt's legendary wealth and hospitality were living up to their reputation.

The journey began in 'Cleopatra's canal' that ran from the harbour at Alexandria through the city's Egyptian quarter, appropriately enough since the trip would take them from the cosmopolitan world of their present into a very different – and for Caesar, eye-popping – world of the past. Sailing across Lake Mareotis, the flotilla entered the Nile proper at Naukratis, nearly fifty miles south of the sea the Romans were beginning to see as theirs.[48] They travelled across the Delta to Khem, which the Greeks called Letopolis, and Iunu, the Greek Heliopolis (Sun City) on the opposite bank. What is fascinating about this journey is how many ancient temples were already tourist attractions to the Greeks and now the Romans. Even as far south as the Valley of the Kings, astonished visitors had chipped graffiti into the mysterious stone blocks – 'I saw and was astonished' was the most common phrase. At Heliopolis, Cleopatra probably took part in the sacred ceremony of the local Mnevis bull, reinforcing her role as protector of her country's religion.

At Memphis, Cleopatra may have been crowned again in the Egyptian tradition with the coiled cobra, the sun disc of Ra and the horns of the sacred cow on her top-heavy crown. She was Nea Isis, the living goddess, and Isis was the female equivalent of Ptah, god of creation, from whom the name Egypt was born.

At various points on this royal progress, Caesar must have been astonished at the 'magic' of the decadent east. Cleopatra's priests used Persian, Babylonian, Jewish and Greek variants of their gods in their elaborate rituals and involved the whole panoply of animal deities – Horus, the hawkhead, whose tears were the most powerful talisman in the ancient world; Anubis the jackal; Bes, the dwarf god of birth; Sobek, the crocodile. At Khmun, the Greek Hermopolis, which was the cult centre of Thoth, god of wisdom, with whom the intellectual Cleopatra had a particular affinity, sacred ibises with their odd-shaped beaks were fed a diet of clover. These birds and the baboons Caesar had probably never seen before were mummified in the area in their thousands.

So impressed was Cleopatra by the appearance of the Ptolemais Hermion that she wrote to Theon, her 'fixer' in the area on 7 March 46 'let the relevant persons be told that the temple of Isis built on behalf of our wellbeing by Callimachos [her *strategos* along this stretch of the Nile] is to be tax free and inviolable together with the houses built around it as far as the wall of the city'.

At Dendera, special songs were written for Cleopatra's and Caesar's visit. 'Pharaoh comes to dance and comes to sing. Mistress, see him dancing, see the skipping!' We have no clear idea of the sound of Egyptian music, although we know what instruments it was played on. This far south, it may have been influenced by the African tribal rhythms of Nubia with its drums and tambourines. The priests and 'events organizers' would have remembered that Cleopatra's father was Auletes, the Piper, with his love of music and drink.

At Thebes, Caesar would have seen the 60-foot-high statues that made their own music, and sang to passers-by. In fact, it was a trick of the desert winds that echoed through the narrow gaps between the statues' legs. Elsewhere, Egyptian priests were not above helping the 'magic' along by chanting from secret recesses in temple walls. The gullible, and this may even include Caesar, believed every word.

We do not know exactly how far south Cleopatra and her lover-god sailed. Caesar was fascinated, as were most scholars then and since, with the source of the Nile, but if finding that was his intention, he came up woefully short. Not for another nineteen centuries would that problem be solved.[49] One account says that Caesar's soldiers would go no further, rather as Alexander the Great's army had once said 'enough is enough' on his campaign trail 300 years earlier. There was clearly no mutiny as such, but Caesar must have realized that his heaven-storming *calligae* had not seen home for six years, in some cases more, and he owed them a comfortable retirement on the farms of the latifundia. More importantly, with Pompey's sons Sextus and Magnus on the rampage in their murdered father's name, he had unfinished business in Rome.

The couple and their dazzling entourage turned north again and made for Alexandria. The general left Egypt on 10 June. He had been away from Rome for six hectic months and he left 12,000 troops behind for Cleopatra's – and Rome's – protection. Some of these men would never see their homes again. Did the trip down the Nile, with its heady mix of divinity and adoration, give him ideas above the station of a mortal Roman, which would lead to his death two years later?

Two weeks after Caesar left, Cleopatra went into labour with her first child – Ptolemy Caesar – the offspring of the two most powerful people in the world; another Alexander.

12

LITTLE CAESAR

ALEXANDRIA, 47

Ptolemy XV Caesar Theos Philopator kai Philomater, the father-loving and mother-loving god, was born on 23 June 47.[50] His birth, though details have not survived, would have followed the same Graeco-Egyptian ritual mix of common sense, wisdom and religious mumbo-jumbo that had surrounded Cleopatra's own birth twenty-four years earlier. The boy had the golden hair of his father, although detractors at the time and historians later have doubted whether Caesarion (little Caesar) was actually Caesar's child. The question must be asked whose child could he have been? Ptolemy XIV was still only thirteen so consummation of his political marriage to Cleopatra must seriously be doubted. We *could* factor in a suitable attendant/slave stud, perhaps Apollodorus, but the time-scale means that

Cleopatra would have to be sleeping with him at the same time as Caesar. What is important is that the three men who mattered most in Cleopatra's life in this time-frame and slightly later – Caesar, Mark Antony and Octavian – all believed Caesarion to be Caesar's. Let that be enough.

For a ritual seven days, mother and baby rested hidden from the world, even from most of the court. Infant mortality was high in the ancient world, as it would remain for centuries, and only time would tell if Caesarion would live to become the new Alexander. The period of greatest danger over, Cleopatra and her son emerged into the Alexandrian sunshine to begin a round of esoteric celebrations. The Nile rose, as if by magic, giving a new birth to the people of Egypt as their queen had to Caesarion. Cleopatra had new coins struck, showing the boy as Horus, the son of Isis, whose living counterpart she was. The legend read *Kleopatras Basillas*, Cleopatra the female king.

In some ways this was the high water mark of Cleopatra's reign, so soon after it had been re-established, and from the pattern of events – the quiescence of both Alexandria and Upper Egypt – she must have been coping well with all the minutiae of government we saw in Chapter 1. Nominally still married to Ptolemy XIV to appease the supposed traditionalists, both Greek and Egyptian, she may well have been hatching plans for a fuller official relationship with Caesar. Depending on how it went for him in Rome, his little son might inherit the earth.

Caesar was not yet in Rome. Traditionalists there wrung their hands. The Republic had been shattered by the war between Pompey and Caesar and was in desperate need of healing. Mark Antony, who had been left behind with

Lepidus to hold things together in Caesar's absence, was becoming an embarrassment. He had been helping himself to Pompey's various properties, including the Alban villa where Cleopatra had stayed with her father as a girl, and doing what Mark Antony did best: drinking. It was rumoured that he staggered around the *tabernae* of Rome with an 'actress' called Volumnia on his arm and even drove a chariot pulled by lions through the streets. Where, wailed the traditionalist republicans, was Caesar?

He was in Anatolia (modern Turkey) in August 47, hunting the sons of Pompey, both of whom had escaped Pharsalus, and getting money out of local rulers who had lent cash to Pompey in the civil war. In terms of payback, nobody was more thorough than Julius Caesar. At Zela on 2 August, Caesar took on Pharnaces, the king of Pontus, who had overrun a section of Rome's rapidly growing empire in the previous months. Pharnaces' chariots, with their scythed wheels, literally sliced through the Roman ranks, but the veteran 6th Legion held the line and drove back Pharnaces' left flank where a steep ravine broke their formation. Caesar sent back to Rome his famous despatch – *'veni, vidi, vici'* – 'I came, I saw, I conquered'.[51]

By the end of September Caesar had crossed to Tarentum in the south of Italy where he met his old enemy Cicero who was there in his villa under house arrest by Mark Antony. Caesar released him in exchange for cash, which cannot have done much to heal the breach between them. Caesar may have been on his way back to Rome at this point – in fact, the visit to Tarentum makes little sense if this was not his plan – when word reached him that Pompey's sons were rebuilding an army in what today is Tunisia.

Back went Caesar to Africa, sailing on the last day of the mid-winter solstice, which the Christians would hijack later as the birthday of Jesus Christ, and reached Hadrumentum three days later. This was not the sailing season and the Mediterranean could be notoriously treacherous, especially around Sicily, but men like Caesar had no patience with such things. By the standards of the ancient world, he was an old man in a hurry.

Gnaeus and Sextus Pompey had perhaps two legions and the crack cavalry of Juba of Numidia, who used elephants and camels to instil terror in the enemy. Realizing that Caesar was unlikely to be beaten in the field, Pompey's sons kept up a guerrilla war until 6 April 46 when Caesar forced them to fight at Thapsus. The Pompeys' army was led by Metellus Scipio who abandoned the relative safety of his fortified city to confront Caesar head on. As at Pharsalus, Caesar's army formed into three lines, but changed formation at the last minute to panic Juba's elephants whose headlong flight caused chaos in Scipio's ranks. Once again, we have the laughable propaganda figures of the victors – fifty of Caesar's dead compared with 5,000 of Scipio's. Scipio himself committed suicide in the Roman tradition, as did Cato (the younger) who had opposed Caesar for years and had fought against him at Dyrrachium. The irony was that the patriotic republican would almost certainly have been spared if he had surrendered because that was Caesar's way.

The conqueror of so many lands and winner of so many battles – 302 by his own account – helped himself to Juba's treasure, absorbed Juba's cavalry into the Roman army and made Numidia a Roman province, rich, as it was, in grain. Fifty-four years old and suffering increasingly from the falling sickness, Julius Caesar went home.

Now the full effect of Caesar's destruction of Pompey became apparent and it began to dawn on the senate that, far from restored in their republican glory, they were being sidelined. It was partly their fault. They heaped increasingly ludicrous honours on Caesar. He was *Pontifex Maximus* again and Dictator, at first for ten years and then for life. He began to wear scarlet parade boots and to dress as the ancient kings did, although he pointedly refused the title of king even when Mark Antony offered it to him. One senator proposed that Caesar be above the law and that any woman in Rome should be his for the asking. In his darker moments Caesar probably realized that if Pompey had been the victor at Pharsalus, he would be approaching a kind of divinity just as Caesar was.

And nowhere was Caesar's arrogance more obvious than in the four triumphs he effectively awarded himself in September and October. The festivities lasted for forty days, during which Rome itself was in chaos. Nobody worked and at various times people were trampled to death in the hysterical crowds. Gold crowns – 2,822 of them: nine tons of bullion – were paraded in the streets from all parts of the empire. Each of Caesar's *calligae* got 6,000 denarii as a bonus (the usual pay was one denarius a day). Generous as this was, one legionary, overheard to grumble that it could have been more if it were not for the cost of the triumphs, was decapitated for his insolence and his head displayed in the Temple of Mars.

The Gallic triumph came first, Caesar riding in his chariot with a slave behind him whispering, 'Remember you are mortal.' Caesar didn't remember it, not at least until the Ides of March two years later. His axle broke, but he was above omens like that and revelled in the adulation of the mob. The procession lasted all day; forty elephants with flaming torches in their trunks lit the bizarre finale, in which

Vercingetorix, the Gallic leader, was garotted in full view of the crowd. Most of them were horrified, not at the spectacle itself, but because Vercingetorix was a brilliant general and deserved a better fate.

The second triumph was for Caesar's victory over the Egyptians. The Nile was portrayed as a huge male god and there was an enormous model of the Pharos lighthouse and paintings of the deaths of the treacherous Potheinos and Achillas. Once again, the crowd were less pleased with the appearance of Cleopatra's sister Arsinoe, bound in golden chains. Caesar had taken her with him when he left Egypt and the crowd probably thought he intended to have her publicly strangled too.

The Pharnaces campaign was celebrated in the third triumph and the last one was for Africa, with grisly pictures of Pompey's supporters, like Cato, committing suicide in their abject failure and misery. The prize here was little Juba, the four-year-old son of the king of Numidia, who would be kept in Rome and brought up as a Roman, the most civilizing of all fates. There were chariot races and gladiatorial combats in which 320 gladiators fought to the death for the crowd. Four hundred lions died in the arena[52] and for the first time, Romans saw a giraffe, which they called a cameleopard on account of its soft muzzle and spotted hide. Pitched battles were re-enacted, even one involving a naval fight on an artificial lake.[53] No expense was spared and Rome loved it.

What they did not love was Cleopatra. Caesar sent for his Greek wife in the late summer of 46, but it is unclear exactly when she arrived in Rome or exactly why he sent for her. Stacy Schiff believes that this was Cleopatra's first visit, indeed her first sailing across the Mediterranean. If, as I believe, she had travelled with Auletes as an eleven-year-old, she was not only used to sailing but knew Rome too. The circumstances were, of course, very different. Then she had been a child, albeit a precocious one, effectively exiled from Egypt and going cap in hand to Rome. Now she was a queen, mature, powerful and sophisticated. She had survived civil war, as Rome had, and not only had a son who would continue her line, but her son's father was the most powerful man in Rome. Now she would come with all the status that went with her position and she brought the proverbial kitchen sink. Effectively the whole court travelled with her. Arsinoe, of course, was already Caesar's prisoner in Rome. Caesarion was brought to show Caesar his son for the first time (which may well explain why he had invited Cleopatra in the first place) and, bearing in mind the Ptolemies' reputation for intrigue, kid-brother and husband Ptolemy XIV was brought along too. It was not safe to leave him behind.

All this makes it clear that Egypt – and more especially, Alexandria – was quiet. Cleopatra would not have dared leave if there were unrest of any kind. In what was an age of intensely personal government, she was not only removing the queen, the living Isis, but her husband-brother and her heir. In fact, if Cleopatra's ship had gone down in the Mediterranean it is difficult to know who would have ruled Egypt, and the Ptolemaic dynasty would have come to an abrupt halt seventeen years before it did. Undoubtedly, the Romans would have moved in and turned Cleopatra's country into a province.

Experts are divided over the travelling time. Stacy Schiff claims that Cleopatra was a nervous sailor, and that the entourage was so huge that the ships could not carry enough provisions to stay in open water and had to put in to various coastal villages in Rhodes and Crete to re-victual. This could take weeks. Joann Fletcher thinks the journey might have been accomplished in less than a fortnight, depending on the prevailing winds. On the other hand, Fletcher implies that Cleopatra was not there for Caesar's triumphs; Schiff believes she was.

The problem is that we have no Alexandrian evidence for this visit, only the occasional reference in Roman writings. Surely, if Cleopatra had been there for the triumphs, Caesar would have paraded her, not as a prisoner of war, which she was not, but as a 'friend and ally of Rome', and this does not seem to have happened. On the other hand, wouldn't the dictator have wanted her there to share his celebrations as he had shared hers along the Nile? Perhaps she watched from under one of Caesar's expensive silk awnings, taking in the spectacle from a discreet distance.

What the real Cleopatra did *not* do, unlike Elizabeth Taylor in 1963, was to make her own triumphal entry into Rome. The film (described in Chapter 18) shows the queen and her five-year-old son (Caesarion was actually about eighteen months old) sitting glittering in gold between the paws of a huge basalt sphinx, the whole float carried by Nubian slaves. Rome would not have stood for that, as both Caesar and Cleopatra knew.

At Piteoli, Rome's nearest harbour, Cleopatra would have been met by Caesar or a delegation. She would have given thanks for her safe sea-crossing at the temple of Isis in the town before travelling by carriage or litter along the Appian Way which, when she was Caesarion's age, had been dotted with the crucified corpses of Spartacus' army.

By Caesar's edict, no wheeled vehicle could be driven in the streets of Rome during the hours of daylight, so

Cleopatra either arrived after dark or was carried by her slaves in a litter. She was housed in Caesar's villa on the Janiculum Hill on the west bank of the Tiber, a fashionable spot with cypresses and cedars and well away from the dictator's town house near the Forum where he lived with Calpurnia. Given the likely size of Cleopatra's entourage, the villa would have been too small and her staff and hangers-on must have been housed elsewhere.

What did Cleopatra make of Rome now that she saw it through a queen's eyes? Probably not a lot. When the British chieftain Caratacus was taken in chains to the city as a prisoner of war in the next generation, he was astonished at the size and splendour of the place. 'Why, with all this,' he is reported to have asked, 'do you want our poor mud huts?' It was a fair question but he never saw Alexandria. Technically, Rome's population was probably bigger than that of Cleopatra's capital, but it was crammed in between those annoying seven hills and was frankly a mess. The only truly impressive buildings in the city centre were Pompey's Theatre and Caesar's Forum, huge physical statements made by the men who had slogged it out for the victor's laurel wreath. Elsewhere, jerry-built houses were falling down or being pulled down by property developers like Crassus, always on the look-out for a fast denarius. For a nation that prided itself on the rigid formality of its army camps and its innate sense of order, Rome's streets were a shambles. Cleopatra's palace back home dwarfed anything that Rome had to offer – and it covered a third of spacious, grid-patterned Alexandria. She probably stayed away from the sweating multitude and waited for the world to come to her.

Cleopatra's presence made life awkward for Romans. Caesar's friends, including Mark Antony and the gauche,

puny sixteen-year-old Octavian, who would become
Caesar's Roman heir, may have been frequent visitors, as of
course (presumably without Calpurnia) was Caesar himself.
The historian Cassius Dio noted that Caesar was not at all
concerned by the malicious gossip that flew in every *taberna*
and on every street corner. Cicero, sixty, bitter, sidelined
and with his beloved Republic sinking into a morass of
corruption and dictatorship, visited Cleopatra more than
once because, like most people, he couldn't stay away. The
Greek woman was fascinating. She was highly intelligent,
could talk literature and politics like any man and had that
dazzling radiance coupled with the magical, musical voice.
In a letter to his friend Atticus on 13 June 44 he wrote:

> I hate the queen...[Her] insolence when she was living in
> Caesar's house in the gardens beyond the Tiber, I cannot
> recall without indignation. So, no dealings with that lot. They
> seem to think I have not only no spirit, but no feelings at all.[54]

There was some carping about a book. It seems from the
letter that Cleopatra had offered to lend Cicero one and had
forgotten about it. He was, of course, missing the point. She
had every right to be insolent – Cicero's father was a minor
landowner and she owned the largest library in the world.

But Cleopatra caused upset in a wider and far more
important context. Caesar put up a golden statue to Isis in
the temple of Venus Genetrix in the Forum. Since Isis was
so closely associated with Cleopatra, the image could have
been of the queen herself. The Egyptians might erect such
statues to living rulers; the Romans did not. One or two
statues of Pompey were permitted, but only after the man
was dead. Rome was outraged but only the shrewdest politicians saw the extent to which Caesar had been bewitched

by the Egyptian whore. He embarked on a series of reforms that autumn, which, far from restoring the Republic, seemed to be turning Rome into an alien place. He set up plans for a great library along Alexandrian lines where Greek as well as Latin texts would be lodged. He set up an official census along Egyptian lines – the birth of Christ is recorded in the Bible as taking place at census time in the reign of Augustus Caesar, the lifted title that Octavian took for himself. Caesar intended to drain the Pontine marshes around the city, deadly as they were with malaria-carrying mosquitoes, to create locks and canals of Alexandrian design. He wanted to turn Ostia into a huge, modern port with quays and docks like those in the Egyptian capital. He encouraged the cult worship of the drunken god Dionysus, with whom Cleopatra's father had been identified, even though Romans hated the idea. He rationalized the calendar, instituting the Julian month and re-ordering the year according to the latest Greek thinking.

All this was modernization and most of it made sense, but it went completely against what Romans loved most – tradition. It all seemed so *foreign* and it could all be laid at the door of Cleopatra.

It is not likely that she stayed in Caesar's villa for two years. Egypt could not spare her for that long. She probably sailed home for the summer of 45, returning later in the year having assured herself that all was well in Alexandria. But on her return, all was far from well in Rome.

Caesar came back from his last campaign in September 45 and wrote his will. Placed in the temple of the Vestal Virgins (which not even the most ferocious rebel was likely to attack), the document stated that his entire estate should pass to his son or any future sons. Caesarion is not mentioned by name (it was illegal for Romans to make bequests to foreigners) but the clause was there because his father knew perfectly well how fragile life was; the boy might not live to adulthood (he didn't) and Cleopatra might yet bear him more sons. Should that fail, three-quarters of his estate should go to his great-nephew Octavian (Gaius Octavius) who, in the event of his own death, would be proclaimed Caesar's son. The remaining quarter was to be shared equally between a nephew and another great-nephew.

As 44 dawned, Caesar may have been starting to think of himself as a god. This was routine in Egypt – for centuries the pharaohs had been revered this way and the Ptolemies had continued the tradition. To diehard republicans, this was the worst thing that could happen. Caesar sat on a gold throne. Caesar had his face chiselled on coins. Caesar was *Pontifex Maximus*. Caesar was Dictator for life. The old checks and balances of consulship, praetorship or quaestorship for a year did not apply to Caesar. Again, on the feast of Lupercalia, Mark Antony offered Caesar the title of king of Rome. Again, Caesar refused, but his refusal seemed, to those who heard it, more hesitant than it had been.

And the last straw was a new campaign that Caesar had been planning against Parthia. With that state destroyed, the way would be clear to India where Alexander the Great's army had gone 300 years earlier. And wasn't the queen of Egypt descended from one of Alexander's generals? And, worse, wasn't there an oracle that had foretold that Parthia could only be conquered by a king?

Rome, 15 March 44. It began a day like any other and it was raining. Later omen-watchers and rumourmongers would claim that lightning bolts struck down statues and lionesses whelped in the streets. Caesar had been warned to beware the Ides of March,[55] essentially a frolicsome drinking festival, and to stay away from the senate. Calpurnia had had a dream in which Pompey's statue ran red with blood. Caesar had already sent sixteen legions marching east and Rome was waiting to hear who he would appoint consul in his own absence on campaign.

He had been at dinner on the previous day when the discussion turned on death and his own answer as to what sort of death was best was 'a sudden one'.

The morning of the 15th was business as usual. In the senate, Caesar sat on his throne and heard petitions. Mark Antony, who might well have been able to save the man's life, was delayed in conversation outside. Tullius Cimber tugged on Caesar's toga as he gave him a scroll to read. This was the signal the others were waiting for. Publius Casca struck the first blow, aiming for Caesar's throat but merely grazing his chest. The Dictator threw him aside but was hit in the ribs, probably by Casca's brother Gaius, who later denied all knowledge of it. The others closed in for the kill, the embittered republican Gaius Cassius Longinus aiming deliberately for the face. Stumbling in his toga, bleeding profusely and dying, Caesar staggered at the base of the statue of his old enemy, Pompey, and recognized his friend (and perhaps illegitimate son) Marcus Junius Brutus, dagger in hand. He said, 'You too, my child?' And he said it, not in the famous '*Et tu, Brute?*' of the Romans, but '*kai su teknon?*' of the Greeks. It was the language of cultured Romans, but it was also the language of Cleopatra.

The honourable men who had murdered Caesar, hysterical and covered in his blood as well as their own where their knives had missed the intended target, spread out from Pompey's Theatre to tell an appalled Rome what they had done. The man who would be a god lay with twenty-three stab wounds and for Cleopatra, any hopes she had of a future with him were shattered. That part of her life was over.

BOOK FIVE: ANTONY

13
REBIRTH

ROME, 44

With hindsight, all the murder of Caesar achieved was a speeding-up of the inevitable. If the honourable men who killed him hoped for an instant restoration of republican values, they were mistaken. Amateurs at the killing game, they had effectively bungled the assassination, had no coherent plan for the future and ultimately let the moral high ground fall to the two men who most of Rome saw as Caesar's successors – Mark Antony and Octavian.

Caesar's mutilated corpse was delivered to Calpurnia. There was panic in the streets. Mark Antony, temporarily wrong-footed, got out of Pompey's villa, which was now his home, and left Rome, disguised as a slave. It was the second time he had done that. We do not know who broke the news to Cleopatra or what her reaction was. Joann

Fletcher has her tearing her hair and clothes in the traditional lament, but this in itself was only a knee-jerk reaction
– all around the Mediterranean, such ritual was expected.
Our problem, for all the bitchy comments of Romans like
Cicero, is that we do not know the exact relationship of
Caesar and the queen. In Egyptian/Alexandrian eyes, she
was his wife; in Roman terms, his mistress. She was almost
certainly the mother of his child (and was, according to
Cicero, pregnant again by the Ides of March). Was she in
love with him? Or he with her? We cannot answer that.
What is obvious is that the death of Caesar represented a
catastrophic political blow to Cleopatra. If she had ambitions to play queen of Rome to Caesar's king, as some
Romans believed, that would never happen now. And it was
not safe for her to stay in Rome.

She probably did stay in Rome for Caesar's funeral, but
took no part in it. While Mark Antony, creeping back after a
suitable time, now launched his 'Friends, Romans, coun-
trymen' to the mob while displaying Caesar's wounds,
Cleopatra's people were packing. By the middle of April she
had gone, sailing directly for home past the Straits of Messina.

As her flotilla sailed past the Pharos light, to be welcomed
probably by her huge battle fleet, Cleopatra must have
realized that, after the shock of the last weeks, all was well at
home. Whoever had run Egypt in her second absence – it
would nominally have been Ptolemy XIV but backed by a
highly competent, if anonymous, finance minister – had
done an excellent job and the queen could relax.

The next three years of Cleopatra's life and reign are
shrouded in a certain mystery. If she was indeed pregnant
when she left Rome, she must have miscarried because if
there was one thing the Alexandrian/Egyptian chroniclers

would have monitored, it was the birth of a royal child, especially if it were a boy, a brother to Caesarion. More likely, this was a piece of malicious gossip, which Cicero, ready to believe anything of the woman who forgot to lend him a book, readily accepted. The summer of 44 would have been one of celebrations. In July Caesarion was officially designated a pharaoh of Egypt – 'King Ptolemy, who is as well Caesar, father-loving, mother-loving god.' He was three, but in the months ahead, his bas-relief would appear in front of his mother on the temple wall at Dendera as a fully grown adult, wearing the crown of both Egypts. In terms of Egyptian art, he is indistinguishable from Rameses the Great or any of the pharaohs of the older kingdoms.

Everywhere, art appeared with Cleopatra as Isis. She was consciously building on the Isis/Horus/Osiris story. Osiris was the murdered Caesar, dismembered by assassins' knives in the senate; Horus, his son Caesarion vowing to avenge his father's murder. Others would do that work for him, but as far as Cleopatra's propaganda is concerned, it was perfect – history repeating theology. A cynical world like ours sees all this as hypocrisy and hype, but that is to misunderstand the woman and her times. Cleopatra's people, Alexandrians and Egyptians, believed all this and so did Cleopatra. It was an integral part of life.

As well as the Dendera temple, Cleopatra began a building programme on a par with that of her father. A new temple sprang up at Edfu to the south and she built a shrine in ship form at Coptos. A birthing-house, which was part chapel, part natal clinic, was established at Armant (Hermonthis). The place had an antechamber, a walkway with columns, two reception rooms and a flat roof for rituals, as well as the birth room itself. Cleopatra was only twenty-six; there may well be other royal births. In Alexandria itself she ordered the construction of the Caesarion, a shrine to her dead husband, with libraries, colonnades and a brilliant art collection. She also began a huge temple of Isis, which would have dwarfed everything else in Alexandria but which was unfinished at her death and was probably never completed.

The intellectual queen returned to her bluestocking interests. The library at Alexandria had always attracted scholars, a university by another name, and Cleopatra encouraged this. Didymus was the most distinguished of these, churning out 3,500 monographs on everything under the sun. So supportive of medical science was the queen that later Arab scholars, who always thought more highly of her than their narrow, prejudiced Christian contemporaries, assumed that she herself carried out studies into gynae-cology and obstetrics. Perhaps she did. A book referred to, but which has not survived, is called the *Gynaecia Cleopatrae* and refers to contraceptive methods that were supposedly used by the queen. The Egyptians of this period certainly used primitive caps made of a mixture of crocodile dung and honey, but we cannot link any of this directly to Cleopatra. It is out of this fascination with burgeoning science that later generations would fashion the legend of Cleopatra the sorceress, skilled in the black arts that could emasculate strong men and unsettle the world.

In the day-to-day running of her country, which is so infuriatingly vague in terms of the written record, we must assume that Cleopatra was coping well. Not to do so would invite revolt, especially in hot-headed Alexandria, which had a reputation for dismembering its rulers. The usual Nile floods of 43 and 42 did not happen. What is explicable to us today as banal geography and weather systems were presumed to be the result of divine displeasure then. No doubt the priesthood, led by Cleopatra as the living Isis, would have gone through the ancient rituals to their gods. But people were starving and on a more practical level, the queen devalued the currency, reducing the silver content of her coinage, for the first time giving coins an actual token value. The bronze drachma she issued was roughly the value of the Roman denarius. She opened the royal granaries, vast, guarded warehouses within the royal compound in Alexandria, and distributed free wheat to her people.

There was a flood of petitions from all over Egypt and invariably Cleopatra granted concessions, eased tax burdens and generally made life as comfortable for her people as she could. The Jewish historian turned Roman sycophant Josephus maintains that the queen did not extend these privileges to Alexandria's large Jewish community. This is unlikely. We know that Jews were involved in all levels of government, even the surprisingly efficient police force, and it was a Jewish army that had backed her and Caesar in 48. This is probably an early example of a Jewish writer heaping misery on his people as of right, a self-fulfilling prophecy that would echo down the centuries. But, then, Josephus, like Cicero, 'hated the queen'. To cap it all, a disease that sounds suspiciously like bubonic plague broke out on Egypt's frontiers, adding to the country's woes. Even so, there was no rebellion, nor even a rumour of one; Cleopatra was doing something right.

But the curse of the Ptolemies was not fully extinguished. If Caesarion was the heir, then Ptolemy XIV was very definitely the spare and as such he may have been in the way. The boy was fifteen in 44 and while Cleopatra took him with her on her second trip to Rome she appears to have left him behind on the third. On the surface all appeared calm when she came back in April, but could there have been machinations from her kid brother? After all, exactly the same thing had happened about six years earlier, when Ptolemy XIII had conspired with Potheinos *et al* to oust Cleopatra. Nothing on that scale happened in 44, but she would have been ultra-sensitive to the possibility, as would her supporters.

Our problem is that we know almost nothing of Ptolemy XIV. His older brother was petulant, emotional, prone to burst into tears and, in the circumstances of his death by drowning on campaign, unlucky. But *this* Ptolemy is just a cipher, a pharaoh in name only. Eleven years Cleopatra's junior, he is unlikely to have had any say in the politics of her reign. He *could*, of course, have died of any one of a hundred natural causes, given the era in which he lived, but the timing is suspect. His death enabled Cleopatra to declare Caesarion as co-regent, something she could not have done during the boy's lifetime. Josephus states openly that she murdered her brother and we all know that Josephus, writing a century after her death, was prepared to believe *anything* of Cleopatra. The balance of probabilities is that she did have the boy dispatched, perhaps by poison, so that the whole thing could be done quickly, without fuss, behind the palace walls. And the motive, rather than the queen doing a bit of tidying up, is that Ptolemy may have been conspiring behind the scenes with his other sister, Arsinoe.

We last saw the girl as part of Caesar's Egyptian triumph back in 46, bound with golden shackles. It is possible that he intended to have her murdered, as the Gallic chieftain Vercingetorix was murdered, but that would have offended the sensibilities of Rome and Caesar knew better. Instead,

she was sent into exile in Ephesus in modern Turkey in what
was probably a loose and not unpleasant house arrest. As a
schemer and survivor, Arsinoe was a chip off the Ptolemaic
old block. She surrounded herself with a growing group of
supporters at Ephesus who demanded she be queen of
Egypt. She almost certainly had agents working for her (as
did Cleopatra) in Rome and may have been responsible for
the appearance of a pretender to the throne, claiming to be
Ptolemy XIII miraculously surviving the drowning in the
Nile delta.[56] This would be ideal; Arsinoe could supplant
Cleopatra and rule with her 'brother', satisfying Ptolemaic
and Egyptian tradition and giving her sole power in reality.

One particular problem area was Cyprus. Auletes' will
had stipulated that Cyprus should go to Arsinoe and
Ptolemy XIV as his youngest children. The place was
important to Egypt because it provided copper and timber,
but Rome had taken it from Auletes' brother and it is likely
that the island never had much affinity with Cleopatra
herself. Rumours reached the queen in 43 that Arsinoe was
in contact with Serapion, the local governor. Both sisters,
however, knew that the only way Arsinoe could make real
headway was by getting the backing of Rome.

Since the murder of Caesar, Rome was a schizophrenic city,
paralysed by its own insecurity. A greyness physically hung
over the seven hills, which may have been the lingering
volcanic smoke of Etna, rumbling away 250 miles to the
south. By 42 the many factions would polarize into Mark
Antony and Octavian allying with Marcus Lepidus as the
second triumvirate hunting down Caesar's murderers, spearheaded by Marcus Brutus and Gaius Cassius whose 'lean
and hungry look' appalled everybody. In the intervening

months, however, it was almost every man for himself and fortunes fluctuated.

One man who emerged briefly was Publius Cornelius Dolabella. The ex-son-in-law of Cicero, he had been a supporter, nonetheless, of Caesar in the Pompey civil war and had fought with him at Pharsalus and Thapsus. He was prone to push the senate to pass laws that suited him personally, such as the cancellation of debts. On Caesar's death, Dolabella suddenly switched sides, claiming to have been part of the conspiracy all along. He detested Mark Antony, as of course did Cicero, but even so, was slippery enough to accept cash from him and as consul, made sure that there was no martyr cult to Caesar in the months following the assassination. In October 43 he left to take up his post as governor of Syria and this brought him indirectly into Cleopatra's orbit.

The queen must have known that the news of the on-going civil war in Rome would affect her sooner or later. She still had three of Caesar's legions in Alexandria and a fourth had been added recently so there were some 20,000 Romans in her capital. It remained to be seen who would approach her first for those troops and in the event it was Dolabella. Only in his twenties, the man had an awesome military reputation. He was a hot-head and hugely popular, an only slightly watered-down version of Mark Antony, and Cleopatra probably thought he was the official face of the new Rome and she had no choice but to comply. If it came to it, 'her' legions were not likely to fight for her against their own people, so she let them go, leaving her kingdom dangerously defenceless. Her own army was big enough to put down internal revolts and in Alexandria she still had the Gabinian bodyguard, but if a Roman army came against her, it was unlikely she would survive. But there had to be a deal in her parting with the legions; Rome must recognize Caesarion as king of Egypt.

Cleopatra's fleet was hijacked by Cassius to whom it defected without a murmur and this can only be explained by the fact that the vast majority of her naval force must have been Roman. Now it was Cassius' turn to ask her for help. Cassius' reputation was not high and during her time in Rome, it is likely that Cleopatra learned of it. He was cruel and vicious, his temper not lessened by the fact that he had been beaten by the slave army of Spartacus when Cleopatra was a little girl. Such slurs on a man's reputation rarely went away. He knew Syria well, crushing a rebellion in Judaea in 52, and he was marching there now with twelve legions at his back. A prime mover in the assassination of Caesar, he had wanted to kill Mark Antony, too, but the genuinely honourable Brutus had stopped him. Brutus believed he was killing an idea, not a man.

Cleopatra hedged. There was plague in her country and famine. This was no doubt true but it would not have precluded her sending more of her formidable fleet if she had wanted to. In the event, Serapion on Cyprus sent Cassius the ships he had and the Romans marched on Laodicia where Dolabella was entrenched. By now it was July 43 and Dolabella was isolated. Beaten and with his troops scurrying to Cassius' standards, Dolabella did what was 'fine, what's Roman', and ordered a soldier to thrust a sword into his heart.

It would have taken Cassius days to reach the Egyptian border and his army was more or less intact. By now he had grown tired of Cleopatra's vacillation and probably guessed that his opponents Antony and Octavian had also asked for her help. Luckily for Cleopatra Cassius, while on the march south received a messenger galloping from Brutus in Greece. Antony and Octavian were on the march. The unlikely comrades had buried their differences and were on the warpath. Reluctantly, Cassius broke his camp and marched north again.

The exact sequence of events is unclear at this point but the fleet earmarked for Cassius was already at sea and Cleopatra was leading it. In fact, she had no intention of giving him any support but probably planned to throw in her lot with Antony and Octavian. Her own personal presence with the fleet cannot be explained any other way. Does it prove, after all, that Cleopatra really did love Julius Caesar, that she was sailing to play her part in the downfall of his murderers? Perhaps not, but it does add to our concept of the queen. The twenty-year-old who had once led her armies on campaign in the desert east of Pelusium was now the twenty-seven-year-old prepared to sail into battle against the mightiest military power on earth. Those historians who point out she was no general have overlooked these events.

In his fascinating book *The Hinge Factor*,[57] Erik Durschmied looks at the turning points in history, the often insignificant things that have shaped the past. It may be that Cleopatra's fleet would have achieved nothing in 43–42, but we shall never know because storms at sea wrecked her ships and she had to run to port for safety. She herself was taken ill and for anti-Cleopatrans this is proof that she was no sailor and half explains her later actions at Actium in 31.[58] Her illness was probably seasickness, by the way, and it was the pounding her ships took that led to her decision to call the whole thing off. In one way, it was the best of all worlds. She had promised to help both sides in the civil war and had not lost a man in battle. On the other hand, she had given away four legions and a fleet, had a second fleet damaged and had endeared herself to nobody.

The heirs of Caesar were an ill-assorted pair. Mark Antony was the gruff soldier, reveller and Jack the lad. He had a cheery disposition and a notorious reputation with women. Handsome and powerful, he grew a beard in mourning for Caesar, which only seemed to make him so much more of a man than Octavian, who was twenty years younger. The man who would become Rome's first emperor as Augustus was only twenty years old in 43 and Cicero at least saw him as a rising star. In various letters from Cicero, Octavian shape-shifts from 'the boy' to 'that heaven-sent young man'.[59] Antony clearly only ever regarded him as the boy.

What Octavian did have, however, was Caesar's name and that, in a Rome prepared to deify the dead dictator, was hugely important. Octavian may have been young, puny and probably a physical coward, but Antony needed him. He also needed Marcus Lepidus, who, in an age when the legions followed a general rather than the abstraction that was Rome, commanded several thousand men that Antony needed to track down Caesar's killers. In November 43, the three men met at Boninia (near today's Bologna) and thrashed out an agreement. Over two days of horse-trading, the second triumvirate was formed. Antony and Octavian wanted vengeance for Caesar, Lepidus wanted money and nobody believed that this three-cornered, self-centred alliance could last much longer than the time it took to defeat Brutus and Cassius.

The excesses of Caesar had left Rome virtually bankrupt and the triumvirate needed money. It also needed to make sure that it would be politically accepted by Rome itself. None of the three had the stature and gravitas of Caesar and those qualities had got him killed. The only way to secure support was to remove opposition so that the senate and the assemblies would rubber-stamp everything the triumvirs wanted to do. So Sulla-style proscription returned to Rome. Each man compiled a list of men he wanted exiled or dead. Staunch republican virtues, large estates, slurs real and imagined, all went into the melting pot of causation. Cassius Dio wrote that the city was full of corpses, which was an exaggeration but the blood-letting had its effect. When Antony and Octavian led their armies to Greece, it was in the sure knowledge that Rome would behave itself under Lepidus until their return.

The highest-profile casualty in the proscriptions was Cicero, who had been a thorn in Antony's side for so long. He was on the point of leaving his villa to take ship to somewhere safe when a centurion caught him, dragged him off his litter and cut off the head of the greatest orator Rome had known. The head and the hand that had written so many anti-Antony diatribes were taken to Antony's house. They arrived while he was at dinner with friends, and his wife Fulvia spat on it and, removing a hairpin from her elegant coiffure, rammed it into Cicero's no longer deadly tongue.

The triumvirs' army landed near Apollonia and marched along the Via Egnatia in Macedon. Antony landed first; if Brutus and Cassius had had the foresight, they could have beaten him before Octavian arrived. The truth was that Brutus had no military experience at all and though it is difficult to measure such things, it seemed that the bulk of Caesar's veterans were with Antony. Despite the Romans' penchant for exaggerating figures, the armies that clashed twice at Philippi in October were the largest ever sent out of Italy. The republicans had nineteen legions and 20,000 cavalry to the triumvirs' nineteen and 13,000 horse. There is a sense that commanding so many men in the field was a step too far with relatively primitive communication systems. Clashes and skirmishes over several days resulted in the first pitched battle in which Antony smashed Cassius' legions and captured his camp. The republican, believing the whole field lost, committed suicide. In fact, Brutus had done well, driving Octavian's troops back and inflicting heavy losses while their commander, ill and probably terrified, was nowhere to be seen.

Three weeks later, Antony forced Brutus to commit again. While Octavian's troops held the centre, Antony's crossed a marsh and hit the republicans in the flank. Like Cassius, Brutus took his own life and Caesar was avenged.

Early in 41, Quintus Dellius, who had changed sides so often in recent years that a fellow politician called him 'the bare-back vaulter of the civil wars', came to Alexandria. He had been sent to ask the queen of Egypt for an account of her vacillation for the last four months and he came on the orders of the triumvir, Mark Antony.

14

THE GENTLEST AND KINDEST
OF SOLDIERS

ROME, 83

The man who would die with Cleopatra was born fourteen years before her, the son of Marcus Antonius Creticus and Julia, sister of Lucius Julius Caesar who was consul in 64. If we only had Cicero's opinion of him – 'In truth, we ought not to think of him as a human being, but a most outrageous beast'[60] – that would be no truth at all.

The actual date of Antony's birth is uncertain, but it was possibly 14 January 83. The Antonii were a distinguished plebeian family but Julia was patrician, the fifth cousin of Julius Caesar, and that gave Mark Antony a foot in both political camps as far as a career was concerned. Since his father, stepfather and grandfather all held senatorial rank and were *quaestors* at various times, it was inevitable that the family should be caught up in the civil war between

Marius and Sulla that in some ways marked the beginning of the end of the Republic. When Marius returned to Rome at the head of an army four years before Antony was born, his grandfather became one of the would-be dictator's victims. Stabbed to death, Marcus Antonius' head was taken to Marius. Such appalling precedents are difficult to forget and may explain in part the fate of Cicero twenty-six years later.

In 72 Marcus Antonius' son (Antony's father) was sent to Crete to control the extremely serious pirate situation there. His fleet was beaten by the Cilicians whose naval warfare was formidable and unimpressed Romans called him Creticus in mockery of a failed campaign. Antony was eight at the time and his disgraced father died on Crete, leaving huge debts and a miserable reputation. Julia married Publius Cornelius Lentulus Sura who became consul in 71 and Antony spent the rest of his childhood years in his house.

As a boy from a well-placed and connected family, Antony would have been groomed for a public career. Apart from the planning of actual conspiracies, such as that which toppled Caesar in 44, much of Roman life was extraordinarily public. Politicians made speeches in the Forum and outside temples; trials were held in the open air. Budding orators – and every politician had to be an orator – would have to prove themselves against large, indifferent or even hostile audiences. Antony would become part of all this, although, despite his famous oration burying, not praising Caesar, he never reached the heights of his grandfather in this respect.

Young Antony would have learned a great deal under a private tutor – Latin and Greek literature, rhetoric, history – and would know the role of the pantheon of minor gods that guarded his home and his life. The lares watched over the hearth; *educa* and *genialis* guided the boy's mind – there was a long list of them.

He also learned to fight, wrestling on the open plain of the Campus Martius, handling the short stabbing sword all Roman soldiers used, throwing the *pilum* (a lance) and riding without stirrups[61] on the four-pronged saddle. Politicians in Rome were expected to be field commanders, too; the Republic expected an awful lot of its leaders – they had to be generals, financiers, judges and events managers. Few men could manage it all.

When Antony was thirteen, his uncle and stepfather were both stripped of their senatorial rank by the censors of 70. It is unclear precisely why and smacks of hypocrisy. Senators were supposed to be impeccable in their personal and private lives, but as we have seen, this was rarely the case. Caius Antonius and Publius Lentulus seem to have been unlucky – two of sixty-four senators who were the victims of what Lord Macaulay centuries later referred to as the ridiculous spectacle of one of society's fits of morality. He was talking about nineteenth-century Britain, but it could equally well have been Rome in the century before Christ.

Despite the existence of his stepfather, technically, on the death of Marcus Antonius Creticus, Antony was the head of the household. The coming of age of Roman boys was not fixed and there is no actual date for Antony's. At some point in his early teens he now wore the *toga virile* of a man rather than the smaller, purple-edged *praetexta* of a boy. He also embarked on a career of debauchery with his friend Caius Scribonius Curio and acquired a taste for wine and women that never left him. Antony wore a thick, short beard at a time when most Romans were clean-shaven and wore his tunic short to show off his powerful legs. All the later images of the man, on busts and coins, show a muscular, thick-set man, completely at odds with the puny Octavian and even the sinewy Caesar. He and Curio worked their way through a succession of courtesans, the well-bred and surprisingly intellectual tarts who were passed around the Roman elite as a matter of course. In that sense, many Romans realized later, Antony's dalliance with Cleopatra was just more of the same.

Just as Antony's family were caught up in the Marius/Sulla convulsions, so were they in the attempted revolt by Cataline. Lentulus backed the man wholeheartedly and in the fallout that followed, was executed for his pains by garotting. Antony was twenty by this time and old enough to be involved, but he seems to have escaped any of the taint and was probably genuinely innocent or someone would have publicly named him. His uncle Caius Antonius was put on corruption charges in 59 and exiled.

That Antony should have survived so far was extraordinary and it may have been his mounting debts that led to his first marriage, to Fadia, the daughter of Quintus Fabius Gallius. Fabius was a freedman, so his family had no political clout at all. It may be that he was rich and that Fadia's dowry had its own appeal to a young man who had so far done nothing with his life as his family crashed and burned around him. It is equally possible that Antony let his heart rule his head. All his life he was attracted to feisty women – perhaps Fadia was simply the first of these.

In politics, Antony associated himself with the briefly rising star that was Publius Clodius Pulcher, who, with his opponent Milo, was taking Roman elections and realpolitik ever further into the gutter. The liaison did not last long; the pair quarrelled (exactly why is unknown) and Antony left for Greece, nominally to study rhetoric but perhaps because financially he could no longer afford to live in Rome.

He was still there in 57 when Aulus Gabinius passed through Greece on his way to take up the proconsulship in Syria. He almost certainly knew Antony already and took him on. Antony was twenty-six by now without any real experience of politics or the army and the exact role that he took on is unclear. A general (which was what, in effect, Gabinius was as proconsul) needed a staff of officers – the *comites* – who were responsible for all the minutiae of logistics for an army in the field. Crucial as these men were, the post had little appeal for Antony who was a 'dash and fire' soldier in the mould of Pompey. So he became *praefectus equitum*, prefect of horse, the rough equivalent of a colonel. As such he would command an *ala*, a cavalry regiment or perhaps two or three together in a brigade. Most modern commentators on Cleopatra claim that Antony commanded Gabinius' cavalry, but this is unlikely in a man with little except keenness to recommend him.

The fighting in which Antony took part is at once complicated and unclear. The Romans found themselves, inevitably, in a country in which they had no rights, in the middle of a civil war in Samaria and Judaea to the south. Near Alexandrion in the Jordan Valley, Mark Antony erupted onto the military scene, impressing everyone with his guts and ability in hand-to-hand combat. He handled mopping-up operations around Alexandrion and was still involved in this when Gabinius received his offer from Ptolemy Auletes to help him get his throne back.

Plutarch, always superficial, says that Antony took Pelusium in the desert east of Alexandria, but the ease with which he did this probably implied that the city surrendered without a fight. This did not prevent Antony and other generals from adding it to a list of battle honours.[62] Appian, always rather romantically inclined, claims that Antony met the fourteen-year-old Cleopatra at this point and that he fell in love with her. Antony was certainly impetuous and impulsive, and Cleopatra probably already perfectly able to flaunt her considerable charms, but both of them had other plans for the rest of their lives.

Gabinius may have been successful in Syria and in putting Auletes back on his throne, but like far too many over-ambitious provincial governors, he had overstepped the mark and had to answer for it in Rome. Sensibly, although it is difficult to see that much blame could attach to him, Antony stayed in Syria. Marcus Licinius Crassus now took Gabinius' place and began his ill-fated Parthian campaign. It made sense for Antony to join him; he was already in the east and had recent military experience whereas Crassus was over sixty and had not led an army in the field since the Spartacus war in 70. In the event, Antony joined Caesar instead.

Thanks to Shakespeare and the actual events that followed Caesar's assassination, we have the impression that Antony had always been the future dictator's right-hand man, as close to him as a son. This is far from the case. The men were, as we have seen, distantly related by marriage and they must, in the small circle that was the Roman *republica*, have met. We do not know why or exactly how Antony approached Caesar, but it is likely to have been that way round. Caesar had temporarily abandoned the cut and thrust of Roman politics for the cut and thrust of brutal warfare against the tribes of Gaul where Antony turned up in 53.

Again, his status and duties are unclear. Given Antony's earlier experiences, he may well have commanded cavalry units, but Caesar does not mention him until the brilliant siege of Alesia in the summer of 52, during which time Antony had gone back to Rome to further his political career before rejoining Caesar on the front line. Adrian Goldsworthy paints a picture of Antony, now thirty and eligible for a quaestorship for the first time, striding through the Forum in the dazzling white *toga candidus* on his way to the sheep pens in which the open voting took place. With him would have been slaves – the *nomenclatores* – who knew anyone who was anyone by sight and would whisper the relevant name to Antony so that he could glad-hand with confidence. This summer, though, it was different. The cracks in the pavement had widened and the street fighting between the thugs of Clodius and Milo delayed the elections for some weeks.

Antony was elected but in an atmosphere of martial law. The murder of Clodius had led a terrified senate to beg Pompey to restore order and this he did by force. It paved the way for Antony's policy later. He watched as a triumvir used his legions to force through the legality of the senate. The time would come in Rome, and it would not be long now, when three power brokers would become one and the senate would not matter at all.

What is telling about Antony's various military appointments is how limited they were. Plutarch and subsequently Shakespeare paint a picture of the middle-aged Antony as a veteran. He is 'the garland of the war', a hugely successful general against Octavian's boyish callowness. There is almost the temptation to put Antony on the same footing as Caesar and Pompey, but the facts speak otherwise. He became Caesar's *quaestor* on his return to Gaul but by 50 he was back in Rome following up his political career.

The first step on this road was to get himself elected, with the backing of Caesar's supporters and Caesar's newly obtained Gallic money, to the college of augurs. Priests in ancient Rome did not have the same gravitas as those of Cleopatra's Egypt. They were political appointments at the highest level, as they remained in the Church of England, for example, until very recently. The augurs, like the Vestal Virgins, had supposed powers of prophecy, reading signs like the weather, bird flight patterns or interpreting rare, inexplicable events. There was no actual spiritual element in all this, but the Romans were superstitious, almost fatalistic people and such omens were important to them. Antony won against Lucius Domitius Ahenobarbus and the post was life membership of what was in effect a very exclusive club of the Roman elite.

Of more importance was the post of Tribune of the Plebs, which Antony obtained next and he became one of ten appointees for 49. This gave the man real political power. He could frame bills that would become law and veto anything he disapproved of in the senate. He would do that twice on Caesar's behalf in the months ahead. With him was Gaius Cassius Longinus, at that stage a Caesar man rather than an embittered and murderous opponent.

Throughout the year, Antony defended Caesar consistently against those who thought that the general had overreached himself in Gaul. Pompey, who had not actually gone to Spain to take up his appointment there, but had wisely stayed on the spot in Rome, was scornful of Antony. To Cicero he wrote, 'What do you think Caesar will be like if he gets command of the Republic, if his weak and worthless *quaestor* acts like this!'[63] Pompey couldn't even be bothered to give Antony his official tribunal rank. He was often drunk or hungover in public and on one occasion spectacularly vomited while making a speech in the senate.

Both Antony and Cassius were waiting as Caesar crossed the Rubicon and marched south. They called the senate to a meeting on 1 April while Caesar waited beyond the city walls with his army. There were few attendees, as we have seen, but the general stayed just long enough to strip the Treasury before marching to Spain. At his back, he entrusted Rome itself to Marcus Lepidus and the rest of Italy to Antony.

Caesar's campaign against Pompey took its toll on Antony's family and friends, even if he was not directly involved. His brother was captured, his cousin killed and his old friend Curio, beaten by Juba's Numidians, was decapitated, his head sent to the king as part of his own triumph. In Italy Antony seems to have lived up to Caesar's expectations. There were no pro-Pompey risings and much of his time was spent fitting out a fleet at Brundisium that would take Caesar to Greece to destroy Pompey once and for all.

It was probably now that Antony remarried. The record is silent on the fate of Fadia. Epidemics were frequent in cities like Rome and she may have died. Equally, Antony could have divorced her (this was especially easy for a man), since the daughter of a freedman was hardly of the right social class for a Tribune of the Plebs and an augur who was now assuming praetorian powers by running the Italian province. His second wife was his cousin Antonia, the daughter of Caius Antonius, but within a year he had divorced her. It is likely that at this stage the real love in his life was the actress Cytheris whose real name was Volumnia. She was a freed slave with a huge talent for dance and music. Like many courtesans, she had been passed around the elite for some years, living for a while with the Marcus Brutus who would kill Caesar three years later.

Unlike Cleopatra, whose personal written word is almost non-existent,[64] we have letters from Mark Antony to Cicero, who was desperate to leave Rome to rejoin Pompey. Caesar had stipulated that no one should leave Italy and Antony's letter is a thinly veiled threat – 'However, because I am so very fond of you … [?] my dear Cicero, I implore you not to make a mistake …'[65] Cicero took the hint and stayed put until Caesar himself came home and released him from his virtual house arrest.

When Caesar embarked from Brundisium on 4 January 48, Antony was left behind again. His task was to raise more troops, since Caesar knew that Pompey outnumbered him. On 10 April, evading Pompey's naval blockade, Antony crossed to Lissus on the Greek mainland with 10,000 infantry and 8,000 cavalry. On joining Caesar Antony was given the post of Legate commanding the 9th Hispana Legion. This unit had already distinguished itself in Gaul and Britain but its reputation had been tarnished in recent months by a mutiny in which the Ninth refused to march until they got their back pay and the definite promise of land on their return. Caesar had put this insurrection down quickly with executions of the ringleaders. It is difficult to know why he gave them to Antony. His own preferred legion was the 10th Gemina, and it may be he needed a stalwart to make sure the Ninth behaved themselves, often on the furthest wing from his personal control on the battlefield. Antony was in the thick of the fighting now. On one occasion the Ninth held a fort against Pompey's superior forces for a whole day before the attack failed and reinforcements arrived.

At Pharsalus on 9 August, Antony commanded the left flank, near the River Enipeus, and although the fighting was hot here – he was facing the Cilician legion with Spanish auxiliaries led by Africanus – the battle was really won, as we have seen, by Caesar on the right wing detaching the fourth line to create a new formation behind the dust cloud of his cavalry.

Back in Italy while Caesar chased Pompey to Egypt, Antony was chosen by Caesar to be *magister equitum*, Master of the Horse. The title continued to carry huge weight in Europe down the centuries and amounted to Caesar's second-in-command at the time. If Cicero was appalled by Antony's behaviour as Tribune, he was outraged now. Caesar's right-hand man swaggered around Rome with a bodyguard or an entourage of pimps and actors and even wore his sword into the senate where such things were just not done. If Antony's intention was to sweeten Caesar's return he was going the wrong way about it.

If Antony had avoided involvement in the street fighting between Clodius and Milo, he landed up to his neck in a similar debacle in 47. Cicero's son-in-law Dolabella stood as Tribune of the Plebs in that year and proposed once again the abolition of all existing debts. Apart from the obviously self-centred nature of this sort of legislation, it is difficult to see what it could achieve for the long-term finances of the Republic. Antony was away from Rome at the time but on his return he marched into the Forum with soldiers at his back and drove Dolabella out. While he was dealing with this potential rising, discontented, unpaid soldiers of Caesar's pet legion, the Tenth Gemina, began to make loud noises in the Campania countryside south of Rome. Like the Ninth, they had not received their allotted land-plots and felt aggrieved about it. Only Caesar's return and his personal intervention calmed them down.

While Antony was busy buying up property abandoned by exiled or dead supporters of Pompey and giving away priceless furniture from Pompey's own villa where Cleopatra had stayed as a girl, he married for a third time. This was Fulvia, already twice-widowed. Since her first husband was Clodius and her second Curio, Antony must have known her for years. Once again he had found a strong woman in the Cleopatra mould. Fulvia was high born and rich, inheriting fortunes from both her parents, and was counted as one of Rome's great beauties.

We have already traced Antony's actions after the murder of Caesar. The weeks and months that followed the Ides of March are tortuously complicated, with leaders rising and falling, allegiances shifting and mob violence in the city spreading to open warfare in the provinces between the Caesarians and Pompeians and every shade of opinion in between; everybody claimed to be fighting for the Republic. In this atmosphere of mistrust and fear, Antony moved from Caesar's Master of Horse to consul in his own right.

It became clear by the autumn of 44 that Octavian, still only eighteen and almost unknown in Rome, was fast becoming a threat to Antony. Both men tried to grab the legions and were only partially successful. Octavian was untried, but he was a Caesar and he promised more cash and land in return for services than Antony did. Such was the state of chaos in this period that Antony went from consul to public enemy (declared so by Cicero's repeated insistence to the senate) and back again. At one point he was defeated in battle – at Forum Gallorum – by the conspirator Decimus Brutus – but the creation of the triumvirate restored his power and status.

Philippi sealed it. It was Antony's greatest victory and it drew a line in the sand under the whirlwind events since the Ides. Among the triumvirs, Octavian had the most difficult job, of sorting out Rome and paying the army; Lepidus, always regarded as inferior and even slightly unreliable by the other two, had Africa. Antony had the east. And in 41 the most important area in the east was Egypt. He sent Quintus Dellius to Egypt's queen, Cleopatra.

15

THE INIMITABLE LOVERS

TARSUS, 41

Antony and Cleopatra's meeting at Tarsus – the future St Paul's 'no mean city' – has gone down in legend. Plutarch pulls out all the stops to describe it; even Shakespeare could do no more than copy him (almost verbatim) and the film-makers have had a field day. Cleopatra had done her homework on Antony. They had first met fourteen years before and although no one mentions it, it is inconceivable that he wasn't one of her dinner guests on more than one occasion in Caesar's villa on the Janiculum Hill. The rest she may well have got from Dellius, who seems to have been enslaved by her as far greater Romans were. She probably already knew that beautiful, powerful women captivated Antony; she knew he liked a drink. What she may have learned from Dellius was that he had recently declared himself to be another Dionysus, aptly underlined by his drunken revels in Rome. What could be more perfect for Cleopatra? Her father Auletes had called himself the new Dionysus and Dionysus was also Osiris in the Egyptian pantheon. She was the Aphrodite who was also Isis. They were already a couple in the eyes of the heavens. And it gave her a clue as to what to wear.

Joann Fletcher waxes lyrical on the range of expensive make-up, especially for the eyes, that Cleopatra had at her disposal. The hair, the robes, the eyelids heavy with yellow saffron or lapis lazuli – all were chosen with great care.

But even before the actual meeting, Cleopatra was playing hard to get. She ignored Antony's letters and even took her time when Dellius turned up. Sailing in state with half her court and the equivalent of the kitchen sink, she may have approached Tarsus from Cyprus, the legendary birthplace of Aphrodite. And that was the message relayed along the coast and up the River Cydnos – Aphrodite was on her way to revel with Dionysus for the good of Asia. The barge she travelled in is the one that Shakespeare lifts entirely from Plutarch (see Chapter 17) and she reclined under a star-glittering canopy while little boys clothed as cupids scampered around her and her maidservants dressed as wood and sea nymphs. The smoking incense from the deck wafted along the river reeds and the sound of rattles and flute music reached Antony in the market-place.

The exact time of arrivals was impossible to predict with all the variables of the ancient world, so Antony may have been genuinely busy hearing petitions in the al fresco Roman style when the queen's barge was sighted. Alternatively, he may have been trying to affect a nonchalant air – after all, he was the most powerful representative of the greatest power on earth and *he* had sent for *her*. If that was the case, it failed badly because the crowd, the supplicants, even Antony's own staff began to melt away to gawp at the sight – surely one of the most exotic in history and the imperator was left virtually alone on his dais.

Not to be outdone, he did not join the adulatory throng himself but sent word to invite Cleopatra to dine with him that evening. She refused and invited him instead. This was a sticky moment of protocol; technically, it was Antony, as the resident, who should have played host. On the other hand, Cleopatra was a queen and, in her own country at least, semi-divine. Antony could call himself Dionysus as often as he liked; he was not a god, just a rather pushy and ambitious man who may have been about to over-reach himself.

Every commentator on Cleopatra expresses themselves speechless at the scale of the banquet. Bearing in mind it happened on her barge rather than in a palace, it was extraordinary and was eclipsed only by those she threw in Alexandria weeks later. On the first night, the company ate off solid-gold plates set with precious stones. The 'crockery', cutlery, goblets, tables, even the couches they sprawled on were sent home as 'doggie bags' with the guests, Cleopatra's slaves carrying it all through the streets of Tarsus. On the second night, it happened all over again. But behind all the conspicuous consumption, there was a hard kernel of realpolitik on both sides. Each one wanted something from the other and if sex was thrown into the mix, so be it.

Cleopatra was twenty-eight by now and Plutarch positively slavers over her as far as a later-generation Graeco-Roman could over a foreigner.[66] She was at the height of her powers, politically and seductively, and some historians have claimed that she ran rings around Antony, her inferior in every sense. In some ways it was an action replay of her bizarre meeting with Caesar, yet in others totally different. Then, the twenty-one-year-old wanted the general's help to restore her to her kingdom and she briefly became his mistress, later his wife in the process. Now she was an accomplished queen and politician, some said sorceress, and she could buy Antony ten times over. The point was not lost on her, though, that she needed the man's support. If he *was* Rome, at least as far as the East was concerned, she wanted him to affirm Caesarion as pharaoh of Egypt and perhaps extract a little more from him. Arsinoe was still at Ephesus, a stirring and potentially troublesome rival; and a man calling himself Ptolemy XIII had appeared, miraculously delivered from his watery grave in the Nile delta marshes.

Antony was forty-two. He had reached the pinnacle of his own success but wanted more. He knew he had enemies in Rome (everybody did) and he also knew it was only a matter of time before the boy Octavian began to muscle in on his domain. What he needed was a brilliant military victory along the lines of Caesar's in Gaul and the obvious way to that was to destroy Parthia. The warlike people in what is today Iran and Iraq had taken advantage of the Roman civil war to claw back lost territory. When Crassus had tried to bring them to heel in 53 they had destroyed him and his legions; they still had the eagle standards to prove it. Caesar had once sent sixteen new legions to take them on – only his assassination had prevented him from leading them. And to make a Parthian campaign a success, Antony needed money. And who had more money than any other single individual in the known world? Cleopatra.

A deal must have been struck during the heady wine mix of the banquet as the lights bobbed on the decks and the slaves danced and played music. Serapion, the *strategos* who had defied Cleopatra and declared for Cassius from Cyprus, was executed on Antony's orders. So was the pretender Ptolemy XIII. It must have been Cleopatra who effectively put Arsinoe's neck in the metaphorical noose. She was worshipping at a temple to Artemis when Antony's hitmen dragged her out and killed her. The Roman was all for slaughtering the temple priests at Ephesus too, since they had willingly proclaimed Arsinoe queen of Egypt, but Cleopatra seems to have urged mercy and he complied. It had not been so many years since Antony had played a similar role to hers in reining in Auletes in Alexandria.

Antony's and Cleopatra's critics have seen in all this her ruthlessness and his weakness. She might just as well have put a ring in his nose like the Buchis bull and dragged him, garlanded and perfumed, to slaughter and mummification. But all this is to miss the point. We have seen already that internecine murder was what the Ptolemies did – they'd done it for 300 years. We cannot see the family from Hell in conventional terms. 'The past', wrote L. P. Hartley, 'is a foreign country; they do things differently there.' So did the Ptolemies. Both parties seem to have got exactly what they wanted out of the Tarsus summit meeting. Cleopatra had no rivals for her throne and her son's continuing rule after her death was assured. Antony got his cash for Parthia.

When Cleopatra sailed home, it was business as usual for Antony. He put down a revolt in Syria before following her to Alexandria. Again, with hindsight we see a pattern – he would do the same thing, fatally, at Actium ten years later. She snapped her fingers and he jumped. In fact, we have no idea who initiated who, but it is likely that Antony was as captivated by Cleopatra as Caesar had been, even though he paused on the way to seduce the wife of the king of Mauretania. It is this sort of high-class power-bed hopping – he had an affair with the queen of Cappadocia just before the Tarsus meeting – that has led historians to doubt whether Cleopatra meant anything to Antony other than another notch on his bedpost. In Alexandria, however, they seem to have become a couple.

Caesar had come to the city as a potential conqueror at the head of three legions. Antony came as a private citizen, wearing Greek dress, going to the theatre and working out in the gym like other virile Alexandrians. He was careful to speak their language, literally and metaphorically. People remembered the handsome commander of the Gabinian cavalry and how he had prevented wholesale slaughter in the restoration of Auletes to his throne.

But if Antony knew how to play to the gallery, Cleopatra was better at it. She indulged him, watching as he wrestled and practised swordplay in the gymnasion. She hunted with him in the desert. She attended the theatre with him. She was there when he talked to the scholars in the great library – and was no doubt tactful enough not to upstage him in the conversation.

The couple came to be known as the Inimitable Livers, the founder-members of an elite drinking club who wined and dined almost nightly, sometimes disguising themselves as slaves and rolling around the streets, pulling faces at passers-by and getting into fist fights. They diced together, they fished on Lake Mareotis and played practical jokes on each other and their friends. On one occasion, with most of the Court bobbing about on the lake, Cleopatra sent a slave underwater to hook a reeking old saltwater fish onto

Antony's line so that the 'great angler' was ridiculed in the eyes of everyone. Unlike Caesar and certainly unlike Octavian, Mark Antony had a great sense of humour and took it all in good part.

It is difficult to believe that Cleopatra was laughing *at* Antony rather than with him. What would be the point? They already had from each other what they wanted politically. The stay in Alexandria can only be interpreted as a genuinely romantic interlude and by the time Antony left for Parthia, Cleopatra was carrying his twins.

Antony's clash with the Parthians was delayed, however. They had invaded Syria in 40 under their king Pacorus and, if unchecked, posed a threat to Cleopatra's Egypt too. The delay came because of the arrival in Greece of Antony's wife, Fulvia and her sons Antyllus and Iulius. Antony's mother was with her too. Time and again in the next five years, Antony would be distracted by other things. Rome called him or Cleopatra did and he went at their behest away from the Parthian objective. In this at least he proved himself not to be another Caesar.

The family had run from Rome because Fulvia had antagonized Octavian so much that the legions she controlled, on Antony's behalf, were now squaring up to each other for a renewal of the civil war. As Adrian Goldsworthy sums up with classic understatement, 'The result was a confusing period of unrest ... in which allegiances were often unclear.'[67] In other words, it was basically the same business as usual since Caesar had crossed the Rubicon. Increasingly in these months, the third triumvir, Lepidus, was sidelined as governor of Africa and there was a smouldering build-up of tension between the other two, which would end in the collapse of an independent Egypt and the deaths of Antony and Cleopatra.

In the fighting, Octavian sacked Perusia, sacrificing 300 of the town's inhabitants to the gods. Sextus Pompey, in the meantime, still a potential threat on the outskirts of empire, called himself the 'king of the seas' and captured Sicily, blockading the trade routes that led to Rome.

Most modern commentators agree that Fulvia's provocation of Octavian came from her jealousy of Cleopatra; that declaring war was the one sure way to bring the wayward Antony home. If that was the case, it didn't work. When husband and wife met in Athens, Antony was notoriously cold, left her weeks later without saying goodbye and did not see her again. She was dead, probably from exhaustion, by the end of the year.

Joined by Gnaeus Domitius Ahenobarbus (Shakespeare's Enobarbus), one of those on the periphery of the Caesar assassination, Antony landed in Brundisium with 200 war-galleys and faced Octavian and his legions. These men were rather happier now that he had given most of their veteran comrades farms, which would come their way too in the fullness of time. Neither side wanted to fight, and an uneasy truce resulted in the Treaty of Brundisium of September 40. The relief, to a nation exhausted and terrified by civil war, was palpable and ironically people were accidentally killed in exuberant street parties in Rome and Brundisium itself.

The terms of the treaty effectively created a duumvirate to all intents and purposes. With Lepidus in Africa, Antony and Octavian divided the rest of the Roman world between them; Octavian had the west which included Rome and Italy while Antony had the east which of course included Egypt.

Octavian promised him eleven legions to take on the Parthians and the new rapprochement was sealed with a wedding. Fulvia's death freed Antony and his new bride was the beautiful and sophisticated widow Octavia, Octavian's sister. She was about thirty and the fact that Octavian gave her to Antony might imply a genuine attempt on his part to bury the hatchet. On the other hand, it could simply have been Octavian's way to keep a close watch on his rival.

At more or less the same time, Octavian divorced his wife Clodia on the grounds that she was a nag and married the much younger Scribonia, despite the fact that she was already pregnant by her former husband. Both triumvirs celebrated orations in Rome late in 39 – an oration was less lavish than a triumph and it was given partly because there was no actual campaign victory to celebrate. It was just a feel-good exercise in public relations.

Octavian's reputation fluctuated during this period. Although ultimately he would emerge as Caesar's sole heir, billing himself, not Antony, as the victor of Philippi and emerging, butterfly-like, as the Emperor Augustus, in 39 he was the man who had still not found enough farms for his veterans and who had annoyed civilians by planting ex-soldiers in their back gardens. When, on top of this, he raised taxation, he was attacked in the Forum and hit by flying missiles. Only the timely arrival of Antony and his bodyguard saved his life. The resulting bodies were dumped in the Tiber.

The Peace of Misenum at the end of the summer reconciled the dangerous Sextus Pompey with the others. He was now officially governor of Sicily, Sardinia and Corsica and became an augur, giving him a status in Rome he had never held before. The truce may have continued uneasily (the rumour ran that at every party and banquet, everybody

carried hidden daggers, just in case) but it gave Antony the
chance, at least, to march on Parthia. And he took Octavia
with him. She would only go as far as Athens. Romans did
not take their women to the battle-zone.[68] They waited for
the spring campaigning season to start by enjoying themselves in Athens. Once again, Antony dropped his conqueror
pose, wore Greek clothes, went to the theatre and became
Dionysus. With Octavia in tow he probably drank less than
he had with Cleopatra, but she joined in the social life and
the pair were hailed officially as 'the beneficent gods'.

What are we to make of Octavia? Because she was
Octavian's sister and he was a master of propaganda, an
odour of sanctity clings to the woman. She was probably as
capable and pushy as Fulvia and possibly as Cleopatra, but
she hid it well as the dutiful Roman wife and seems to have
supported Antony all the way, an increasingly difficult job
as he and her brother went their separate ways. Was she, like
Fulvia, trying to tie Mark Antony to Rome by supplanting
his Alexandrian love? And were they lovers at all in the real
sense? The 'Inimitable Livers' became the 'Inimitable
Lovers' in some versions but intimacy is not recorded. If
Antony and Cleopatra exchanged letters (which seems
likely) they have not survived and without them the exact
nature of their love is difficult to measure. Antony seems to
have been an opportunist in love as he was in politics and
war. He was not known to have turned any woman down,
especially one with brains and power to add to their charms.
It is likely that when with Cleopatra he was blissfully happy.
And when he was with Octavia he was happy too.

We know that, this time, Cleopatra kept a watchful eye on
Antony. She sent an Alexandrian staff back to Rome with

him, including a soothsayer who prophesied that Octavian's 'karma' would always outshine Antony's as long as the men were together. Only in distance would Antony have a chance. Was this music to Antony's ears – the soothsayer knowing he had plans to invade Parthia? Or was this prophecy on the orders of Cleopatra, to bring her lover back to the East as quickly as possible? Only one account says that the links between them were more direct – they exchanged letters. Either way, because we do not know their exact relationship, we cannot know how Cleopatra reacted to news of Antony's marriage or the birth of Octavia's two daughters by 37. It is unlikely that she sulked and stormed as Shakespeare would make her do sixteen centuries later. She, above all, understood the nature of political marriages – she may have been married to her father, was certainly married to both her brothers and was now 'married' to her son.

And in October 40, Cleopatra Thea Philopator gave birth to twins, Anthony's children. Octavia may have two girls, but they were single births. Cleopatra had achieved that rarity among the Ptolemies – a boy and a girl born on the same day. All sorts of omens and prophecies chimed with this, from Greek and Egyptian religious tradition. She called the boy Alexander Helios, Alexander the Sun, in honour of the great half-founder of her dynasty, whose embalmed body still lay in the Soma in Alexandria. The girl she named Cleopatra Selene, after an earlier Ptolemy and linked clearly with the moon.

There were celebrations throughout her lands at the delta and along the Nile; adoration and sacrifice at Dendera where the twins were carved on the temple walls; worship of the Apis bull. The vital religious ingredients of Cleopatra's political life went on as before. Not even the death of her high priest at Memphis, Pasherenptah III, broke her stride. His seven-year-old son Petubastis took over his duties. He was the same age as Caesarion and Cleopatra could hold sway over the two boys who represented her earthly and her divine existences.

She made overtures in this year to Herod of Judaea who had fled to her court in the oncoming advance of the Parthians. She offered him, according to one account, command of her army, so highly renowned was he as a general. In the event he turned her down and offered his services to Rome where he led Roman legionaries to victory against the Parthians along with Antony's grizzled veteran Publius Ventidius who smashed his opponents in a series of dazzling victories at the Cilician Gates, Mount Amanus and Gindarus.

But Antony was not there and more importantly, neither were Octavian's promised legions. In the autumn of 37 Antony sent for Cleopatra again. The city of Antioch lay on the River Orontes and was the Syrian capital. A centre of trade, it was famous for its olive oil and wine, both locally produced. It was 15 miles from the sea so Cleopatra and her entourage would have weighed anchor at the port of Seleucia, named after Alexander the Great's general, whose family had ruled this part of the mighty empire 300 years earlier.

Antony and Cleopatra had first met here eighteen years before when he was a junior cavalry officer and she was a fourteen-year-old princess-in-waiting. Here, in 37, Antony met his twins for the first time. The family lived in the palace and it was here that the couple were married. Technically, both were committing bigamy, but there was a great deal of precedence for that in the Ptolemy family and in Roman terms, the now-deified Julius Caesar had done exactly the same thing – and with the same woman! Since Roman law did not recognize marriage to a foreigner, it could be said that Antony had found a loop-hole in legality he could drive a chariot through. We do not know exactly what form the marriage ceremony took. Joann Fletcher gives the options, including the dress, hair preparation and jewellery involved. The simple Roman version was a choreographed seizure of goods – 'So, darling, I seize you.' The Greek version was more delicate – he was Antonius, she was Antonia, although she never used the name; it was the equivalent of today's Mrs Mark Antony. There would have been an exchange of vows and rings and a wedding feast on a scale befitting the union of Aphrodite-Isis and Dionysus-Osiris. They issued coins as joint rulers, which were struck at Damascus and Askalon as well as Antioch.

But the greatest wedding present of all was the one that Antony gave to Cleopatra. He gave her back all the ancient lands of the Ptolemies before Rome took them, something he did not have the right to do. Cilicia, Syria, Phoenicia, the Lebanon and Iturea were restored to her, and Cyprus, Crete and Cyrenia affirmed as Egypt's. Antony drew the line at Judaea, probably because Herod, based in Jerusalem, was a militarily useful ally to Rome. She did, however, obtain a monopoly in the trade of the legendary Gilead balm, a perfume rarer than gold and all the bitumen from the Dead Sea region, which was vital for Egyptian embalming customs.

When Cleopatra went home in the spring of 36, she was carrying her fourth child. She travelled back to Alexandria overland, on a royal progress that took in Herod's Jerusalem. The man was an Arab and his Jewish people hated him. Although there is no evidence for the massacre of the innocents as described in the New Testament, he did kill one of his wives, three of his own sons, an uncle and a brother-in-law. Cleopatra and Antony overrode him in a religious controversy with the tribes of Israel and it turned Herod into a bitter opponent, to add his invective later to join Octavian's. According to Josephus, who, as we know, had his own agenda in the context of Cleopatra, Herod heroically rebuffed her attempts to seduce him and even toyed with having her poisoned.

In September the queen gave birth to Ptolemy Philadelphus, brother-loving, and his eldest brother, Caesarion, now eleven, was named official co-ruler with Cleopatra to celebrate the new arrival.

Since Cleopatra had been given her throne back by Caesar in 48, she had had twelve years of relative happiness. The sun shone literally and metaphorically on her reign in Alexandria. If she had been the richest woman in the world before 37, she was doubly so now and she had four healthy, loyal and adoring children to carry on the Ptolemy line. She also had a dynamic, mercurial lover, but Antony was tied by an umbilical cord of duty to Rome. And somehow, whenever Rome was mentioned, storms arose in 'their sea' and war-clouds gathered.

Antony may have had 100,000 men with him as he marched on Parthia, the largest single Roman army ever seen. Plutarch suggests sixteen legions as well as 10,000 cavalry from Gaul and Iberia. Client kings flocked to him as he marched. They had clashed with Rome before and for most of them, it was an experience they did not want to repeat. This gave Antony 6,000 Armenian cavalry and 7,000 infantry with a possible 30,000 of both arms from other nations. From later events we know that he had enough archers and slingers to keep the Parthians at a respectful distance. At first all went well, but as he reached Media (today's Azerbaijan) he was betrayed by the Armenian king Artavasdes. Antony should have known better than to trust this man – Crassus' head was kicked around on stage during his wedding celebration in 53. Somewhere in the desert, Antony's huge supply train was destroyed by the deadly Parthian horse-archers and he was trapped in Media itself.

The Parthian army relied heavily on its cavalry and despite Antony's *alae* auxiliary units, the real strength in his army lay with the Roman legions, the trained veterans. The triumvir may have faced up to 50,000 horse-archers on this campaign, expert bowmen who fired their short bows from the saddle and under the animals' necks and were particularly dangerous when retreating – the deadly Parthian shot. The Parthians' heavy cavalry were extraordinary – lancers riding heavily armoured horses that would not be seen on European battle-fields until the fifteenth century, by which time gunpowder could destroy them. These cataphracts were unstoppable in Antony's day. In a forced retreat that foreshadowed the even grimmer one by Napoleon from Moscow in AD 1812, Antony fought his way back to Antioch in the middle of winter. His column marched in hollow square formation to fight off cavalry attacks so the legendary speed of the legions (perhaps 20 miles a day) was reduced to four or five at best. His men died from exposure, hunger and dysentery, the universal enemies of fighting men in every age, and he lost an estimated 20,000, between a quarter and a third of his force.

Cleopatra hurried to him at Leuce Come, near the old Phoenician city of Sidon. He had almost certainly summoned her for a third time, but for the first time Antony was in trouble. She sailed in the teeth of winter with food, clothing and money for his army and brought her man home to Alexandria. Antony was exhausted. His own courage and the lengths he went to to rally his men and to care for them were extraordinary (Octavian could not hope to match that) but in the end he had failed, almost as badly as Crassus. But Crassus had died and Antony had come home – or at least to one of his eastern homes. It is likely that at some point on the retreat from Media he had contemplated suicide.

In the spring of 35, Octavian's promised troops arrived at last, but a mere 2,000 rather than the 11 legions and only 70 rather than 130 ships (the rest had been lost fighting against Sextus Pompey off Sicily). And Octavian sent his sister, too. Most historians see this as the final, disastrous turning point in the always fragile relationship between Antony and Octavian. Cleopatra's critics claim that she went on a hunger strike, threw tantrums, sulked and screamed to get Antony back, but this does not sound like Cleopatra Thea, the most powerful woman in the world. If it was intended to be a straight choice engineered by Octavian, it can't have been much of a contest for Antony. He sent Octavia home from Athens without seeing her in person, keeping her troops and her ships, and renewed the Parthian campaign from Antioch. By the summer of 34, Artavasdes was a prisoner, appearing chained in a later triumph and Armenia had been conquered. To celebrate all this, Antony and Cleopatra embarked on a series of celebrations known as the Donations of Alexandria. Antony's critics – and by now there were many of them – claimed that he was trying to emulate a triumph, which could only be held in Rome, but Alexandria had been holding its own celebrations when Romans still lived in mud huts along the Tiber. It is probable that nothing on this scale had been seen before, even in the triumphs of

Roman generals. Antony was dressed as Dionysus, with his ivy-leaf headgear. Cleopatra, in black and gold, was Isis, and the whole city dazzled. In the more formal part of the ceremonies, Antony transformed himself. He appeared now in the breastplate, helmet and cloak of a Roman imperator, with the eagles of the legions around him. He made brilliant speeches in Greek to the politicians and the crowds, and the children were crowned to honour the occasion. Two-year-old Ptolemy Philadelphus was Lord of Phoenicia, Cilicia and Syria. He wore Greek boots and a crown like a little Alexander and no doubt had been coached to walk steadily, as befitted the occasion. Alexander Helios, six, was given Media, Parthia and Armenia and was officially called 'king of kings'. He was betrothed to the Queen of Media on the same day. His twin, Cleopatra Selene, became queen of Crete and Cyrenia.

Over all of them, because of their ages, Cleopatra ruled as regent as Cleopatra Thea Neotera Philopator Philopatris – the new Thea, father and fatherland loving. The Latin legend on her coins struck in this year read '*Cleopatrae reginae regum filium regum*' – Cleopatra, queen of kings and her sons who are kings.

Yet none of this was actually to happen, at least not for long, because of Antony's and Cleopatra's decision concerning her eldest son, Caesarion. He was already her co-ruler, Ptolemy Caesar, king of kings. Now, he was officially declared the heir of Julius Caesar. He was not a Roman citizen and had no following in the city itself, but for the first time, Antony's co-triumvir was made painfully aware of a rival who might, in time, challenge him.

Over 1,200 miles away in Rome, Octavian, Julius Caesar's other heir, vowed vengeance.

16
THE SHARERS IN DEATH

Antony and Cleopatra continued to organize the East, live in splendour and enjoy each other's company. His eldest son, Antyllus, joined them and was taught alongside Cleopatra's children in the rigorous Alexandrian schooling that she herself had undergone. Conspicuous consumption was the couple's trademark. On one occasion Cleopatra, at a banquet, was said to have taken off a large pearl earring and dissolved it in a goblet of wine, for a bet. Scientists of our time have gone to the lengths of trying to reproduce this vanishing act; it doesn't work, except by cheating and crushing the pearl first, which would rather have taken the edge off the magnificent gesture. The man who stopped her from throwing in the other earring, Lucius Munatius Plancus, joined in the nonsense by dressing as Glaucus, the sea-god, complete with blue body paint and a fish's tail. The drunkenness went on, the parties went on. And it rubbed off on the children. Antyllus once gave away an entire set of gold tableware to a young tutor who had pleased him at a dinner party.

The family were hugely generous, as they could afford to be. The only document to have survived that may contain Cleopatra's handwriting refers to a massive tax exemption to Antony's general Publius Canidius Crassus in 33, allowing him the free importation of wheat and wine to Alexandria. The single phrase *'ginestho'* in Greek reads 'let it be done'.

But behind the general lifestyle, the daily administration and the sacrificial duties, a storm was gathering. Although no one had the stomach for it, the civil war was not actually over, however Octavian might pretend to the contrary. It could have been possible to re-order the Republic with a dictator for the West (Octavian) and a dictator for the East (Antony) but Roman minds did not see it that way in the first century BC. Above it all floated the growing shadow of Cleopatra. She was supposed to be a client king, *subservient* to Antony; *and* she was a woman. The stories drifting west with every merchant ship and official envoy said the opposite. *He* was in thrall to *her*, whether by magic or his own weakness hardly mattered. And because of this, Antony was playing precisely into Octavian's hands.

The two men had never been friends but from 33 onwards, the mutual sniping got worse. Octavian accused Antony of drunkenness (he may actually have been an alcoholic by now) to the extent that Antony wrote a defence of his behaviour – *De Sua Ebrietate*, On his drunkenness. He could hardly retaliate; like Julius Caesar, Octavian drank little.

When Octavian began to hurl sexual jibes, however, Antony could throw the mud back. One of the few letters of his to have survived (albeit as a paraphrase from Cicero) reads:

> Why have you changed? Is it because I'm screwing the queen? Is she my wife? Have I just started this or has it been going on for nine years? How about you – is it only [Livia] Drusilla you're screwing? Congratulations, if when you read this letter you have not been up Tertulla or Terentilla, Rufilla or Salvia Titiseniam or all of them. Does it really matter where or in whom you dip your wick?[69]

It is not clear whether these women were actually Octavian's mistresses or merely generic female names, implying that anything in a *peplos* would do for Caesar's heir. Rumours about Octavian's rapaciousness needed no additions from Antony. On one occasion, he is said to have whisked away the wife of his host at a banquet and returned looking mightily pleased with himself while she was dishevelled and blushing.

Far more important in this letter is the phrase *uxor mea est* – she is my wife. In the context in which Antony uses it, it is probably a rhetorical question rather than a statement. But that was part of what had changed Octavian. Antony was free to take any mistress he liked, but to *marry* a foreigner and place her on so high a pedestal was indefensible. And Antony knew it.

Whatever else he was – manipulator, lecher, coward – Octavian was a past master at propaganda. Antony made it easy for him, but in Rome, Caesar's heir was busy building his image for the future. He began to build – and Romans were always hugely impressed by the physical symbols of power – even starting the library Caesar had wanted to build having seen Cleopatra's at Alexandria. He did not talk now of rebuilding the Republic, which most far-seeing men knew was broken for ever. Now, he styled himself the successor of the divine Julius – and halfway to a god himself. There was a deep irony here – all her life, Cleopatra had enjoyed this status, precisely one which Romans found so noxious.

In February 32 so pushy was Octavian becoming that the two consuls, Ahenobarbus and Gaius Sosius, ran to Antony while Octavian figuratively buried his former colleague (Antony had officially renounced his triumvir title) by reading his will to the senate and anybody who cared to listen. According to tradition, Antony was believed to have placed a copy of the will with the Vestal Virgins in Rome, but since it was only Octavian who had seen it and who was able to quote chunks from it, it is highly likely that he had written it himself. Caesarion, the will said, was Julius Caesar's son and heir and Antony left various bequests to his children with Cleopatra. This was illegal under Roman law but the most damning indictment against Antony was that, irrespective of where he died, he wanted to be buried with Cleopatra in Alexandria.

It was only a short step from that libel to the myth that Octavian spread that Cleopatra intended to 'dispense justice on the Capitol'. In other words, she and Antony would oust Octavian, shelve for ever the lie of the Republic and preside as lord and lady, king and queen, over a Roman empire. A second rumour, which rather made nonsense of the first, was that Alexandria and not Rome would become their headquarters. If Antony and Cleopatra were happy enough in the east, why go to such dangerous and unprecedented lengths of taking the west as well?

Octavian showed his greatest skill in turning a renewed outbreak of the civil war, a rather sordid power struggle between him and Antony, into a foreign war, little short of a crusade against the weak, debauched east where women urinated standing up and people worshipped gods with animals' heads. At this stage, the senate was split. Of the 1,000 members, perhaps 600 sided with Octavian, the rest unwilling to believe all the invective about Antony. Historians today argue that if Antony had struck quickly when Octavian's tax hikes to pay for the forthcoming campaign made him unpopular in Rome; or if he had landed *without Cleopatra* in Italy, he could have overthrown his rival and perhaps Marcus Antonius would have become Rome's first emperor.

But that was precisely the point. Cleopatra was the sticking place. Antony now officially divorced Octavia and told her to take herself and her children out of his sump-tuous villa in Rome's suburbs. She went dutifully, willingly, an excellent propaganda tool for her brother; she was the perfect, wronged, Roman wife. From now on, Antony went through the motions of preparing for a war he clearly did not want to fight. Like a sleepwalker, he went through the last months of his life in a curious slow motion – and all of this, both at the time and since, was blamed on Cleopatra. While she was contributing vast sums to the war and 200 galleys to bolster Antony's war-fleet, while troops were being raised as far north as Thrace (today's Bulgaria) and the client kings and their armies were summoned, the lovers dallied on Samnos, watching plays and throwing parties! They held court at Athens where Antony had once lived and Cleopatra was hailed as a goddess as Octavia had been not long before.

By the end of the summer, Octavian felt he had enough support to declare war formally on Cleopatra. He snatched up a *pilum* dripping with sacrificial blood – he claimed this was an ancient custom, but had probably invented it as a powerful symbolic act – and hurled it from the steps of the senate towards the south-east in the direction of Egypt.[70] If ever there was a contrived war, this was it. The traditional method of declaring war was for the senate to demand restitution for a wrong. It would wait for a few weeks for a response, then send an emissary to the enemy's capital to begin proceedings. None of this happened in the case of Cleopatra and, unlike a number of client kings who had shifted sides with the blowing of the wind, she had remained loyal to Rome. Even when given the hopeless choice of which Rome to support during the post-Ides ferment, she had clearly dragged her feet so as not to offend either side more than she had to. For his part, Antony was charged with fighting alongside 'the Egyptian [*sic*] woman against his native country'.[71] The senate officially took away his consulship.

Still Antony did not hurry but steadily built up his war effort. Canidius Crassus joined him with sixteen legions, but none of them was likely to have been up to full strength. According to Plutarch, he had 100,000 infantry and 12,000 cavalry and to his standards flocked the client kings of the east, from Thrace, Cappadocia, Mauretania, Armenia and Greece itself. Herod of Judaea was sent to deal with the Nabatean Arabs who were not paying their allotted tribute of bitumen, although this decision may have had something to do with Cleopatra in that she clearly hated the man and he her.

For weeks Antony dithered over what sort of campaign he wanted to wage. He had fought in Greece before under Caesar against Brutus and Cassius and had been successful, but there is always a sense with Antony that he was a better tactician than strategist and the broad brushstrokes of war are the ones he was less good at applying. Despite the Parthian debacle, he was popular, experienced and knew the country. Octavian, with a similarly sized army, was fighting on foreign soil (his presence at Philippi had been very nebulous) and he was strapped for cash to keep his campaign going.

Antony had vast resources from Cleopatra. Not only did she provide a large proportion of the fleet, but most of the galley rowers were Greek or Egyptian and she literally spoke most of the languages of the client kings, keeping them on-side with her well-known charm offensive. She seems to have been less charming to Antony's Roman generals. The gruff Ahenobarbus, once an anti-Caesarian republican, was now one of Antony's most loyal supporters, but he clearly found the queen's presence in Antony's tent offensive. He called her 'Cleopatra' to her face and followed none of the fawning flattery a queen of her wealth and power was due. Late in the day, he abandoned them both and went over to Octavian, dying shortly afterwards, probably of malaria. Dellius deserted too, although given his track record, this could have been predicted. More serious was the defection of Lucius Plancus, who had once been a cringing courtier, dressed as a fish for Cleopatra's delight. Not only did he leave the pair in the lurch, he took Antony's war plans with him. It is one of the great unanswered questions why Antony did not see this as a pressing need to change them.

Octavian's ace-in-the-hole was Marcus Vipsanius Agrippa, a long-time friend and supporter of the triumvir, whose fleet (actually Cleopatra's fleet) had smashed that of Sextus Pompey off Sicily. He was a gifted military commander and probably the best admiral Rome produced.

He had recently been *aedile* responsible for Octavian's building programme in the city, but his first love was action at sea and he made the opening moves of the war, striking at the port of Methone, the most southerly of Antony's outposts. Antony was wrong-footed. He had prepared too slowly and expected an initial attack further north. His fleet at Methone was captured, reversing the ship numbers in Octavian's favour and King Bogud of Mauretania was killed trying to defend the town. Octavian landed and occupied the town of Torone, which means ladle. It also means penis in Greek slang and Cleopatra quipped that it made no difference that Octavian was sitting on his ladle – he'd been doing that for years. Such ribaldry only added to Rome's low opinion of her and disguised the seriousness of the situation. Once Octavian had landed on the Greek mainland, the focus of the campaign became the Gulf of Ambracia and particularly Actium on its seaward side. When Antony arrived from Patmos he was outnumbered so refused to be drawn into a land battle straight away. He had already offered to face Octavian in a personal duel but the result of that would have been so obvious that the triumvir declined. Within days, Antony's cohorts had arrived and he offered battle. Again, Octavian refused. Conjectural history is always difficult – the 'what ifs' are rarely decisive – but it seems likely that if a pitched land engagement had been fought at that stage, Antony would have been victorious and Octavian's gamble would have failed. As it was, Antony languished in a malaria-infested swamp for sixteen weeks before attempting a break-out by sea.

Cleopatra was criticized at the time just for being there and even modern commentators regard her as being at best in the way and at worst countermanding Antony's strategy with ill-informed female illogicality. Little of this makes sense. She was not a general, say her detractors, yet she had camped with Achillas in the desert outside Pelusium before visiting Caesar in Alexandria; she had led her fleet in action against his murderers. As queen, she must have felt it was her place to command her troops in person; it was what the Ptolemies did. Against that we have only the Roman bigotry, which said that women had no place in an army camp. It was the kind of thinking that allowed Boudicca of the Iceni to destroy three Roman towns in Britain before the legions finally stopped her.

At first, Antony had a camp within bow shot of Octavian's on a narrow peninsula between the Ionian Sea and the Gulf of Ambracia. As malaria, low morale and desertions took their toll, he abandoned that and established himself at a base in Acarnania, across the narrow gulf entrance from the enemy. There were skirmishes and clashes in which neither side gained an advantage. Against the advice of Canidius, who advocated marching inland and drawing Octavian after them before tackling him on ground of their choosing, Antony opted for a naval break-out, which would still allow a rearguard to escape by land. They could all reform in Alexandria, with fresh troops, high morale and no malaria. That alone makes sense of what happened on 2 September as the trumpets announced the emergence of Antony's fleet.

Naval battles were not the fast, long-range artillery duels of steel, engine-driven ships. The largest ships in either fleet were the huge war-galleys with ten banks of oars. Antony's flagship was one of these – so, probably was Cleopatra's *Antonia*. Most of them were quinqueremes or triremes, driven by five and three banks of oars respectively. We have no clear idea of the ethnic make-up of the rowers, but the vast majority would have been slaves and they were shackled to their oars with chains. Each ship had a single mast and one sail, but in battle, the oars did the talking, building up to ramming speed at which the bronze-tipped beaks at the prow would smash into the timber mid-ships of the enemy. Artillery would fire rocks and burning balls of pitch onto enemy decks as the galleys closed and then grappling irons were thrown to lash the ships together. Boarding parties of legionaries would jump from wooden towers and fight as if on land. Most of Antony's troops were not used to warfare of this kind and in keeping with most men at the time were unable to swim. Both sides had their ships in a three-block formation, but by September Antony had had to destroy at least eighty of his ships because he had insufficient crew to man them. Against him, the centre was commanded by Lucius Arruntius; Agrippa had the left wing and Caius Lucius the right. Octavian was with this wing (on land, commanders-in-chief usually occupied this position) but he was curiously indisposed on 2 September and Agrippa co-ordinated the battle. For two hours or more, neither side gained advantage, but Antony's manoeuvring meant that large gaps had appeared in Octavian's line and through one of them sailed the queen of Egypt and her lover, heading south under full sail.

The fullest account we have comes from Cassius Dio and he is in no doubt about what happened:

> Cleopatra, whose ship was riding at anchor behind the battle lines, could not endure the long hours of uncertainty while the issue hung in the balance: both as a woman and as an Egyptian [sic] she found herself stretched to breaking point by the agony of the suspense ... Suddenly, she made her choice – to flee – and made the signal for the others, her own subjects.[72]

Nothing about the account makes sense yet until recently it was universally believed. It is simply a piece of propaganda. Dio was writing years later in praise of Octavian who, as Augustus, could do no wrong. Cleopatra's own subjects were Greek as well as Egyptian and there must have been Romans on board, too. They were not directly in the firing line, being well behind Antony's battle stations, and could have rowed back into the safety of the gulf or to land at any time. The fact that Cleopatra signalled to other ships and the fact that she had sails on board the *Antonia* at all, implies that this was a planned move. Antony wanted to fight elsewhere. He would have to clear Agrippa's ships out of the way first – hence the battle of Actium – but then Cleopatra led the way through the gaps he had created and the whole fleet was to follow. Agrippa, without sails, would not be able to catch them.

But something seems to have gone wrong and it is probably all about timing. This is one of those imponderables. A great general has an innate sense about these things – exactly when to hold steady, change formation, fall back, send in the cavalry. Communication from ship to ship was problematic and engagements difficult, at sea, to break off. The fact that Antony had to swing across to a quinquereme from his own flagship implies that Cleopatra had gone too early or that he was too committed against Agrippa's wing. Either way, the result was chaos and Canidius's land troops could only look on in horror as Agrippa's ships closed in on Antony's fleet and an appalling hand-to-hand slaughter took place. Javelins flew at close quarters, grappling hooks smashed into timbers and held fast. Fire hurtled through the blue of the Ionian sky to sear Antony's ships and Antony's men. 'Their corpses were burned,' wrote Dio, 'on board the ships as though they were on a funeral pyre.'[73]

For the next eleven months Antony and Cleopatra adopted a bunker mentality in an attempt to salvage what they could of their empire. There were highs and lows – moments of relief and optimism occasionally puncturing an over-arching sense of gloom and defeat. In this respect, Cleopatra emerged the stronger character. As we have seen already, Antony did not handle defeat well. After Parthia, his confidence shredded, it took him nearly a year to recover; after Actium, he never did. Cleopatra, however, planned, organized, executed. She was the arch-survivor and never more so, ironically, than in the last months of her life.

On board the *Antonia*, sailing south, he sulked and sat on deck, brooding. She won him over, to join her for meals and in bed. In Alexandria, he had a summer-house, the Timonium, built on a jetty in the harbour and lived with a small staff there for weeks before moving, at her cajoling, back into the palace. Cleopatra returned from Actium as though from a victory, the band playing, flags flying and the decks strewn with flowers. What she needed was solidarity and cash and she carried out Roman-style proscriptions of her own. Those who would criticize her once the extent of the defeat was known were executed and their property became hers. No one doubted that Octavian was on his way, if only because the divine Julius had done exactly the same thing in 48 – chased his beaten rival Pompey to Egypt. Cleopatra set about rebuilding her shattered fleet while Antony, in one of his rare moods of optimism, organized his four legions from Cyrenaica.

The pair gambled that Octavian, despite his huge numerical advantage (Canidius' legions had defected en masse after Actium), would not risk the sea or a campaign, however one-sided, in midwinter and that bought them time. Caesarion was feted at a Greek coming-of-age ceremony in Alexandria to celebrate his sixteenth birthday. Antony's son Antyllus officially put on the *toga virile* of a man at about the same time. The message was clear – Caesarion would rule on as the mother-loving pharaoh after Cleopatra's death and Antyllus would one day make speeches in the senate as consul and rule the East as Antony now did.

Both Antony and Cleopatra sent regular letters to Octavian and he replied to most of them. Antony usually employed bluff, reminding his former colleague of their wild youth in Rome. Cleopatra still played the 'friend and ally of Rome' and at one point sent Octavian her royal throne of gold, her sceptre and crown. Symbolically, she was surrendering, but it would be surrender on conditions. She wanted her children to rule Egypt after her. Antony was finished. He had no cards left to play. Cleopatra, with her kingdom intact and a vast personal treasure to which she had recently added, was another matter. It was clearly Octavian's game plan to annex Egypt, take the treasure and bring Cleopatra in golden chains to Rome as part of his triumph, much as Arsinoe had appeared for Caesar years before. Antony would have no role in this. Beaten and discredited as he was, the people of Rome were fickle at all levels of society; the last thing Octavian wanted was a sudden upsurge of sympathy and perhaps even support for the ex-triumvir.

In a surreal schizophrenia, Antony celebrated his fifty-third birthday at the end of January with huge expense, just like the parties of the good old days. On the other hand, and more or less at the same time, the Inimitable Livers became the Sharers in Death, bonded together in a suicide pact that would cheat Octavian of his ultimate victory at the last moment.

With the summer of 30 came Octavian's invasion. Caius Cornelius Gallus marched from Cyrenaica in the west where Antony's legions promptly surrendered to him. Octavian approached from Syria in the east and Pelusium fell without a struggle (although Octavian later told tall tales of his personal heroism in a pitched battle). Antony was faced with that nightmare, a war on two fronts and he did not have enough troops to split his command. He tackled Gallus first and was beaten back by sheer numbers. Undeterred, he struck east, clashed with Octavian's cavalry and forced them back. One particularly brave soldier was commended to Cleopatra in the palace that night and she gave him a breastplate and helmet inlaid with silver as a mark of her appreciation. In the small hours, he defected to Octavian.

The last stand came on 1 August. Antony's tiny fleet sailed out heroically against huge opposition. Within artillery shot of the enemy, they raised their oars clear of the water, a sign of surrender. On land, Antony's cavalry broke formation and trotted across to the other camp. Only his infantry stayed steady and they were quickly defeated.

This whole scene unfolded before Antony and Cleopatra as if in the ghastly slow motion of a nightmare. She had already begun the building of a two-storey mausoleum and had it stored with as much of the royal treasure as it would hold. She said goodbye to her staff and, with only her handmaidens Iras and Charmion, locked herself in the still-unfinished building. She sent word to Antony that she was dead.

From this point on in the narrative, uncertainty mixes with fiction and we are left with messy scenes and loose ends that remain untied. With Octavian's troops pouring into the city, Antony finally decided to end it. He had

contemplated suicide before, perhaps even tried it. Now he
believed his lover/wife was dead, he saw no reason to stay
alive. Caesarion and Antyllus had been sent away for their
own safety and Octavian might yet take pity on the younger
children. Antony asked a bodyguard, Eros, to kill him but
the man refused and rammed Antony's sword into his own
stomach instead. So Antony followed suit.

Death by stomach wound is rarely instantaneous. In fact,
victims have been known to linger for days. Either
Cleopatra was told what had happened (through a locked
door) or it is just possible that she had actually seen it from
an upstairs window and commanded that the dying Antony
be brought to her.

She refused to unlock the mausoleum door so attendants
used a builder's apparatus to haul him up on wooden planks.
With difficulty, the three women got Antony inside and he
died, with all the delicious possibilities for later novelists
and film-makers, in her arms. She screamed and wailed,
tearing her chest with her nails so that the wounds became
infected in the days ahead. She lost her appetite and was
running a temperature, but she had not shared in death yet
and was still trying to get what she could out of Octavian.

The new conqueror of Egypt sent first Caius Proculeius,
then Gallus, to talk to the queen. He wanted her country, he
wanted her treasure (before his huge troop members became
mutinous) and he wanted her alive. To that end, while Gallus
kept Cleopatra talking through the locked door, Proculeius
scrabbled up a rope and in through a window, just in time to
prevent the queen from stabbing herself. There seems to
have been a lull in the negotiations, during which Cleopatra
had access to her doctor, Olympus, and it was now that she
met Octavian for the first time.

The problem is that we have two differing versions of Cleopatra's last days. Plutarch says one thing; Dio another. Both were writing long after the event and both presumably embroidered for the sake of a good story. Dio's Cleopatra is ill, dishevelled and desperate. She read Caesar's faded letters to Octavian and stroked fondly a marble bust in her chamber. Plutarch has her still the proud queen, haughty to the end. When she listed the treasures she owned for Octavian's benefit, a self-serving attendant butted in to add various items she had 'forgotten'. She grabbed his hair and slapped him across the face several times; this sounds like the Cleopatra of old, the hard edge showing in the place of the wide-eyed seductress. Dio's account is most interesting – Octavian could not look her in the face and appears most embarrassed in her company. Plutarch has the nonsense that Cleopatra tried her 'magical' seduction on him, but that Octavian was far too fine and noble to fall for that. And that doesn't sound like Octavian at all.

On 10 August, Cleopatra visited Antony's body for the last time. Romans and Alexandrians usually cremated their dead; Egyptians embalmed them. It is clear from this that some kind of embalming process was used on Antony, as it had been on Alexander the Great, otherwise there would have been nothing to visit. That night Cleopatra, Iras and Charmion had their last meal together and she wrote a last letter to Octavian. Then all three killed themselves.

In what has been described as a classic locked-room mystery, Octavian's guards were sent clattering through the palace (he was probably only rooms away) and found Cleopatra dead, lying in state in the robes of Isis, all black and gold. Iras lay on the floor beside her and Charmion, adjusting the queen's gown for the last time, was dying.

Furious, Octavian sent for the *psylli*, Libyan snake charmers who, it was said, could detect snake venom in a wound by the smell and were expert at sucking it out. For 2,000 years, the asp has been blamed for Cleopatra's death and it is patent nonsense. The only marks on Cleopatra's body (apart, presumably, from the still-infected scratches on her breasts) were found on her arm, implying a pin prick. We know that Cleopatra knew her potions and she also had Olympus on hand to provide a range of poisons. There is no mention of the convulsions and vomiting that cobra bites cause. The poison was probably an opium derivative, which leads to lethargy, coma and respiratory collapse. No snake, not even a six-foot adult, can be relied upon to kill three people so quickly. Iras and Charmion had been handling Cleopatra's combs and hair pins for years – how difficult would it have been to lace any one of these with a deadly toxin?

'Was this well done of your lady, Charmion?' Octavian's guard asked.

'Very well,' she answered, 'becoming a queen descended from so many kings.'

Did she say it? Perhaps not, but she should have done.

BOOK SIX:
THE LEGACY OF CLEOPATRA

17

'YON RIBAUDRED NAG OF EGYPT'

LONDON, AD 1607

History, it is said, is written by the winners. And in 30, that meant Octavian. Such was the brilliance of his rewriting of history that to some, Actium is the last battle in the ancient world; Cleopatra was not only the last Ptolemy and the last pharaoh, she was an anachronism, a seductress with delusions of grandeur that had no place in Octavian's brave new world.

Antony was air-brushed out of history altogether, his eldest son, Antyllus, was decapitated, his younger children brought up by his fine Roman ex, Octavia, who cared for them as if they were her own, not Cleopatra's. Antony's statues were destroyed, the Donations of Alexandria ignored. In Octavian's official account of Actium, there is no mention of Antony at all. But two things of the living Dionysus did survive, both of them beyond Octavian's reach. His silver coinage, with the thick neck and bruiser's nose prominent, were still currency in Rome's eastern empire two centuries later. And, with less felicity, three of his descendants became emperors – Nero, Caligula and Claudius, a trio of the most flawed individuals in the history of Rome. Octavian could not possibly match that.

Octavian's first job in 30 was to secure Egypt. He had coins struck with a crocodile motif and the legend *Aegypta Capta*, Egypt Captured. From now on, it would not be a fabulously wealthy client kingdom to be wooed and flirted with, but a full part of the Roman Empire; in fact, Octavian's personal fief. The huge amount of money it generated paid his troops and turned Rome from brick to marble; the inflation rate was said to have dropped from 12 per cent to 4 per cent almost overnight. Almost everything we see in the city's ruins today owes more to Cleopatra's Alexandria than to any other influence. Octavian left the country to be governed by Gallus as *praefectus*. There was little trouble. Sensibly, Octavian allowed the Alexandrians full mourning for their queen and permitted her the rites of burial alongside Antony. Such trouble as there was came briefly and the revolt was easily crushed by Gallus. When Egypt's fatal lure affected him too and he began erecting life-size statues of himself, Octavian had the senate censure him and the prefect was obliged to follow Antony on the point of his sword.

Cleopatra's imagery remained, not because Octavian had any serious respect for her but because he was aware that in Egypt she was the living Isis and the statuary and bas-reliefs of queen and goddess were indistinguishable from each other. Much more surprising is that her influence spread to Rome where a certain amount of 'Egyptomania' caught on. Whereas Octavian left Egypt in 29 never to return, denouncing the sacred Apis and Buchis bulls as mere animals, the mummified Ptolemies as a load of old bodies and, according to legend, snapping off Alexander the Great's nose by accident during his sightseeing, he brought Cleopatra back to his own city.

His own triumphs – he milked the occasion, turning what was at best two campaigns into three – featured Cleopatra's children and vast heaps of her treasure. Gold, silver and ivory dazzled in the sun along the Via Sacra. The ten-year-old twins, labelled as 'Sun' and 'Moon', were paraded, along with (probably) six-year-old Ptolemy Philadelphus, although he disappears from the record soon after and may even have died (of, probably, natural causes) before the triumph. Cleopatra was there as well – a life-size wax image of her complete with asps coiling up her arms; the legend of her death was already established.

In the wake of this, statues of females appeared all over Rome. The first of these, in Cleopatra's own lifetime, were of Livia and Octavia, but they were erected as an *antidote* to the queen and the idea took off. I am less happy with Stacy Schiff's contention that Roman women received a certain amount of liberation because of Cleopatra, enjoying a far freer hand in business and even politics. Roman *men* still called the shots and would continue to do so for as long as the Roman Empire lasted. And these men began to rewrite history before her embalming process had been completed. Dellius had gone to her as an ambassador and probably had fallen under her spell. Lucius Plancus certainly had, dressing up as a sea-god to please her. The tutor Nicolas of Damascus had taught the queen's children; yet all three turned on Cleopatra and added to the corrosive drips from Octavian's own pen. The poets jumped on the bandwagon. Quintus Horatius Flaccus (Horace) had fought against Antony at

Philippi but he was restored under Octavian and eventually became a sort of poet laureate. In his *Odes*, written about seven years after Cleopatra's death, he enshrined the snake legend. Cleopatra was:

> plotting wild destruction to our Capitol ... a woman mad enough to nurse the wildest hopes and dark with Fortune's favours ... Yet she, seeking to die a nobler death, showed for the dagger's point no woman's fear, nor sought to win with her some swift, fleet secret shore ... courageous, too, to handle poisonous asps, that she might draw black venom to her heart ... no craven woman, she![74]

Publius Vergilius Maro (Virgil) was of an age with Cleopatra and was, like Horace, very influenced by the Greek poets. By the mid 20s, he was working on the *Aeneid*, recounting the adventures of the Trojan prince Aeneas after his escape from burning Troy. En route Aeneas meets Dido, the queen of Carthage, and becomes enslaved by her. The parallels with Antony and Cleopatra were obvious and Octavian took a special interest in the poet and his works.

Sextus Propertius came from Assisi in Umbria and his family lost land in the proscriptions that followed Philippi. Unlike Horace and Virgil, however, he had enough cash not to need a patron, so is less slavishly keen to praise Octavian and damn his enemies. Some experts have seen in his poetry dedicated to a mistress called Cynthia the same dilemma that Antony faced, if we accept that his, in the end, is a love story.

Then the historians took over. We must remember that the writing of history as we know it is a new discipline. The ancient historians often had little to go on – suspect stories distorted by time; a complete lack of understanding of archae-ology; often powerful patrons who paid them to write from a certain perspective; even the need to make a tale tell a moral story. Above all, they were Roman, born into a world dominated by Rome and dominated by men. Cleopatra simply did not fit the bill, so they called her *fatale monstrum*, which is almost untranslatable in its horror. She was unnatural.

Lucius Cassius Dio held various minor magisterial offices in Rome early in the third century AD and his *History of Rome* ran to a vast eighty-volume work over twenty-two years. Although Greek, Dio toes the Roman party line, but his summing-up on Cleopatra has never been bettered – 'She captivated the two greatest Romans of her day and because of the third she destroyed herself.'[75]

Both Appian and Gaius Tranquillis Suetonius wrote of Cleopatra, but both wrote long after her death (in the case of Appian two centuries later) and both were content to add uncritical scraps of gossip to the fuller accounts of Dio and Plutarch. Mestrius Plutarchus was a Greek philosopher born two generations after Cleopatra, but at least he travelled to Egypt and knew something of its culture. His *Parallel Lives*, written about AD 100, paired up famous Romans with Greeks as a moral instruction, a sort of I-told-you-it-would-end-in-tears about the past. Antony is teamed up with the now almost forgotten Demetrios Poliorcetes of Macedon and Caesar with Alexander the Great. Cleopatra appears in those pages of his and has been paraphrased or quoted in this book. Additional material was said to have been obtained from accounts of Cleopatra's doctor, Olympus, but they have not survived.

The oddest – and most biased – of Cleopatra's quasi-biographers is Titus Flavius Josephus, the Jew turned Roman collaborator born about AD 37. Notoriously inaccurate in much of what he wrote, he was convinced that

Cleopatra had treated the Jews of Alexandria badly and painted her accordingly. In his *Against Apion*, he wrote:

> She destroyed the gods of her country and the sepulchres of her progenitors and while she had received her kingdom from the first Caesar, she had the impudence to rebel against his son [Octavian].[76]

Only a quarter of this sentence is correct – she did indeed receive her kingdom from Julius Caesar.

In one last respect, Octavian, perhaps unwittingly, paid a back-handed compliment to Cleopatra. He wanted to begin again. Pretending to have restored the old Roman Republic, that was the last thing he wanted. On the other hand, he knew perfectly well how Rome regarded kingship – the very idea of it had cost Caesar his life. So he became known as first citizen – *princeps* (chief) and took the name Augustus. It means more than wise, it means venerated, elevated, spoken of in hushed tones. The idea came from Lucius Munatius Plancus, who had defected from Antony shortly before Actium. And he in turn took it from Cleopatra Augusta – the wise, the venerated, she who is spoken of in hushed tones. Once, the Romans had stolen Ptolemy's eagle standard and made it their own. Now, they stole a Ptolemaic title and pretended it was theirs too.

Cleopatra's own family probably died out during the first century AD, although it is not possible to prove it. Her daughter, the twin Cleopatra Selene, the moon, married King Juba of Mauretania in 25 and the couple ruled over a watered-down Alexandria at his capital of Iol, which they renamed Caesaria. As a little boy he had appeared in Caesar's triumph to mark the African campaign. Caesarion was murdered with the connivance of his tutor, Rhodon, anxious to ingratiate himself with Octavian. And gradually, those who remembered Cleopatra died and the stories that passed from fathers to sons lost a great deal in the telling and gained fictions of their own. The cult of Isis, banned from Rome by Augustus, may well have lasted in Egypt until the fourth or even fifth century AD but it was eclipsed by the invasion of Islam in 640.

So it was that Islamic culture resurrected Cleopatra. There had been no revolts during her reign and she had never threatened to topple an idea, as the Romans had claimed of her. The Arabic scholars of the Middle Ages could look at the queen in a more detached and positive light. They highlighted her scholarship, her generosity to her people, her extraordinary building programmes. All around them in Egypt, as in other areas the Muslims conquered, the ruins of Octavian's occupation were crumbling into sand.

In Medieval Europe, Cleopatra is largely absent. Until, that is, she undergoes a remarkable transformation. In 1380, the English poet and civil servant Geoffrey Chaucer included her in his *Legend of Good Women*. This was the third longest poem that Chaucer wrote. Like many of the officials who ran the Roman Republic, the comptroller of wines and woollens only did that as his day job; his heart lay with poetry. '*Incipit legenda Cleopatrie, Martiris, Egipti regine*', Chaucer wrote. 'Here begins the legend of Cleopatra, the martyr queen of Egypt'. He apologizes because he does not have the space or time to give detailed descriptions (the whole poem is unfinished) and he merely says of Cleopatra's physical appearance '... she was as fair as the rose in May'. His description of Actium is better, but he could have had no real notion of ancient naval battles and, perhaps unconsciously, seems to be describing the English naval victory over the Franco-Genoese fleet at Sluys off the coast of Flanders a few years before he was born – 'shearing hooks and grapnels full of chains' fill his pages and the use of quicklime, not to mention shelled peas being thrown onto decks to make them slippery! He is in no doubt that Cleopatra ran at Actium, but the soft soul in him says that that was hardly surprising, given the terrifying situation she was in. At her death, in Chaucer's version, she leaps into a snake pit and dies 'for love of Antony who was so dear to her'. Cleopatra died as a martyr to love and in case we are in any doubt, Chaucer writes, 'And this is truth of history; it is no fable.'

The Italian poet Dante, by comparison, perhaps more aware of his 'Roman' pedigree, sees her as a villainess, fit only to be included in his circles of Hell. Her sin, to Dante, was lust. The Italian's allegorical poem, the first part of his *Divine Comedy*, has Dante guided through Hell by Virgil, so immediately the bias of the Roman poets is carried on down the centuries. Cleopatra is one of the 'carnal malefactors' whose uncontrollable libido leads to punishment. She and the others were blown about by fierce storms, never able to rest. Dante clearly had it in for the Ptolemies, since the ninth circle of Hell (Cleopatra is in the second) includes the Ptolemy who ordered the murder of Simon Maccabeus and, according to legend, ordered the trampling of Alexandrian Jews to death with elephants!

The Renaissance was a conscious attempt by European scholars to recreate the lost civilizations of Greece and Rome and so Cleopatra was reintroduced to a whole new generation. Michelangelo Buonarotti made a pastel sketch of the queen. Her broad nose and thick lips make her look very African, showing his complete ignorance of the woman, and her hair coils with asps, like a sultry Medusa. Jacques Amyot translated Plutarch's *Parallel Lives* into French in 1559 and Thomas North did the honours in English twenty years later.

In her excellent *Cleopatra the Great*, Joann Fletcher makes one reference to William Shakespeare – 'Although many biographies of Cleopatra begin with the woman, then examine the way she has been portrayed in later centuries from Plutarch via Shakespeare to Hollywood, this approach can often reveal more about subsequent cultures than about hers.' This is probably true, but *all* subsequent biographies do that – the existing climate and culture of the writer/historian is inevitably daubed all over his/her work and each generation will have a different take on the past.

Much of what we think we know about Cleopatra comes from Shakespeare, who in turn lifted it from Plutarch. Allowing for the passage of fifteen centuries and the inevitable bias of a Romanized Greek author writing about one of Rome's enemies, much is lost in translation. But then again, much is gained.

'Age cannot wither her', wrote Shakespeare, which is precisely why you are reading this book now. 'Custom cannot stale her infinite variety', which explains the various facets of Cleopatra's character that this book explores. Shakespeare's brilliance lies in his ability to capture the essence of his heroes and heroines while adding a magic of his own.

In a bizarre link, 'Egyptians' were well known on English roads in Shakespeare's day. They were 'wretched, wandering wily vagabonds' whose swarthy faces were painted red and yellow. They wore turbans and claimed to be descended from ancient Egyptians, hailing from a 'country which anciently outvied all the world for skill in magic and the mysterious black arts of divination'.[77] Notorious for theft while claiming to tell fortunes, an Act of Parliament was passed against them in 1530 and others followed. Ben Jonson, the playwright contemporary of Shakespeare, wrote a play about them in 1621 – *Masque of the Gypsies Metamorphosed* – which was presented to James I. 'Gaze upon them,' wrote Jonson, 'as the offspring of Ptolemy, begotten upon several Cleopatras in their several centuries.'

Shakespeare had plundered Roman history before, most notably in *Julius Caesar* (1599). In a sense, *Antony and Cleopatra* (1607) is a sequel, continuing the political story of the Republic that was about to turn into an Empire. But it is also a love story and in that sense harks back to *Romeo and Juliet* (1594–5). Even their confused suicides are similar. Antony and Cleopatra are as 'star-crossed' as Romeo and Juliet, in that they come from opposing states, Rome and Egypt, rather as the Italian pair belong to the rival houses of Montague and Capulet. Both couples, in the Shakespeare version, die for love, but Antony and Cleopatra are middle-aged, worldly wise and more cynical.

As with all playwrights in the Elizabethan/Jacobean era, Shakespeare's major problem was how to tell a realistic love story with boy actors in the female roles. Presumably contemporary audiences were used to this (females were not allowed on the stage by law) but passion was a difficult emotion to portray in the circumstances. Shakespeare himself was aware of the problem, putting a rather Zen concept into Cleopatra's mouth when she says 'the quick comedians extemporally will stage us and present our Alexandrian revels. Antony shall be brought drunken forth and I shall see some squeaking Cleopatra boy my greatness in the posture of a whore.' Shakespeare's Cleopatra is a gypsy and a temptress, and the theme that runs through the play is that Antony could have been the greatest Roman who ever lived if he hadn't let himself be seduced by her. 'The beds in the East are soft,' we are told, although elite Romans like Antony hardly lived a spartan life. And Egypt's softness and decadence is contrasted constantly with 'what's fine, what's Roman'.

In this context, an unflattering portrait of Cleopatra – the 'ribaudred nag' (obscene mare) is his line – is maintained by Antony's cynical lieutenant Enobarbus (Gnaeus Domitius Ahenobarbus) who is so disgusted by Antony's infatuation that he deserts him for Octavian. Historically, as we have seen, defection was almost Ahenobarbus' stock-in-trade but Shakespeare ignores this and gives Enobarbus' stand a heroic quality. To fine Romans like him, Cleopatra is 'cunning past man's thought'; 'we cannot call her winds and waters, sighs and tears; they are greater storms and tempests than almanacs can report'. Some audiences may have been appalled that Antony could leave the noble and loyal Octavia, every inch a Roman matron, for a foreign slut.

And it is Cleopatra's influence on Antony that makes him behave the way he does. In *Julius Caesar* he is described as 'a masker and a reveller' – a playboy of the Western world who can quite easily, we can believe, transfer his interests to the East. He and Cleopatra wander the streets at night, dressed as peasants, stumbling from pub to pub. He is consumed by her, neglecting his duty and allowing power to slip to the cold, calculating Octavian.

Only when the Egyptian fleet is defeated at Actium – and that because Cleopatra's war-galley sails away, causing a rout – does Antony realize the error of his ways. In a particularly petulant (and again, unRoman) outburst, he screams at her, 'This foul Egyptian hath betrayed me ... Triple-turned whore, 'tis thou hast sold me to this novice [Octavian] and my heart makes only wars on thee...'

To be fair to Shakespeare's Antony, he is aware throughout the play that he is letting the (Roman) side down. 'A Roman thought hath struck him' in Act 1 Scene II, and when Antony receives various messages from Rome, especially of the death of Fulvia, he acknowledges that 'I must from this enchanting queen break off' and 'These strong Egyptian fetters I must break or lose myself in dotage'.

Cleopatra comes across as fickle and wilful, even childishly awkward when it comes to her relationship with Antony – 'if you find him sad,' she says to her maid, Charmion, 'say I am dancing; if in mirth, report that I am sudden sick.' There is no doubt that theirs is a real love-match – 'Eternity was in our lips and eyes, bliss in our brows' bent; none our parts so poor but was a race of heaven ...' But the pressure of international politics forces Antony into a political marriage with Octavia. Cleopatra is at once broken-hearted and furious at this news and nearly kills the messenger who brings it.

The contrasting images we have of Cleopatra come from the queen herself and from Enobarbus, who for most of the play is playing devil's advocate on Cleopatra's behalf. On a personal level, she describes herself as 'my old serpent of old Nile', which she says is what Antony calls her and describes a middle-aged has-been. 'Think on me that I am with Phoebus' amorous pinches black and wrinkled deep in time'; and this is four hundred years before scientists became aware of the damage caused by over-sunbathing!

Enobarbus, it is true, is more concerned with the outward appearance and the glittering opulence of the Egyptian court. When prompted by the gossip-hungry Romans

Maecenas and Agrippa from Octavian's camp, he tells them of the banquet at which eight wild boars were eaten by only twelve people and embarks on the famous description of Cleopatra's flagship:

> The barge she sat in, like a burnish'd throne burn'd on the water. The poop was beaten gold; purple the sails and so perfumed that the winds were love-sick with them. The oars were silver, which to the tune of flutes kept stroke ... For her own person, she beggared all description; she did lie in her pavilion – cloth of gold tissue – o'er picturing that Venus where we see the fancy outwork nature. On each side her stood pretty dimpled boys, like smiling Cupids ...

Shakespeare's own audiences, of course, had no idea what an ancient Egyptian looked like and found nothing incongruous about mention of a game of billiards in the play. The boy who played Cleopatra in 1607 would have worn a stomacher and farthingale as wealthy ladies of his own day did. Antony would have worn the plate armour of the Jacobean knight and flourished a cup-hilt rapier in the warlike bits. This tradition continued, both on the stage and in art. A painting by Guido Cagnacci in 1658 shows Cleopatra applying the asp to her arm (Shakespeare seems to have invented the bite on the breast). She has red-gold hair (which may be accurate) and the heavy, pale-skinned body of a Rubens beauty. Her throne is pure Italian 1650s. A drawing of Elizabeth Younge as Cleopatra in 1773 shows her in the low-cut bodice and high headgear of the fashionable European courts of the *ancien régime* – she could easily be Marie Antoinette, queen of France.

Not until the late Victorian period do we see any real attempt to get the costumes right. Frederick Leighton, most famous of the nineteenth-century painters who produced vast canvases on Roman history, shows her in her barge, smouldering seductively under an awning beneath the famous purple sails. There is a nod in the direction of Eastern promise in the photographs of Ellen Wallis as the queen in the Theatre Royal, London, in 1873, and something vaguely exotic at the Princess's Theatre seventeen years later when Lillie Langtry played her. By 1906, Constance Collier's outfit at His Majesty's is really very authentic, based on the archaeology that was then being carried out in the Valley of the Kings. Her Antony, the tragedian H. Beerbohm Tree, looks magnificent in the cuirasses and lion-masked cloak that only Hollywood would outdo a few years later.

While Shakespeare's legendary status grew in the eighteenth century, one playwright decided rewrites were necessary. Part-time actor and man-about-town Colley Cibber gave *King Lear* a happy ending (!) and even tinkered with *Richard III*, but in 1724 he wrote his own *Caesar in Egypt*, which is best forgotten. It was *Antony and Cleopatra* in the First Folio format that stood the test of time and the legendary Sarah Bernhardt played her in a variant called *Cleopatre* in the Theatre Porte St Martin in Paris in 1890.

Enter George Bernard Shaw. It would be difficult to imagine a greater contrast between him and Shakespeare or the cultures for which they wrote. Shakespeare's England was about to embark on a 300-year imperial adventure of which Shaw's was the apogee. *Caesar and Cleopatra* was written in 1898 when the British empire was the largest in the world and included what had once been Cleopatra's Egypt. The play was written specifically for the Shakespearean tragedian Johnston Forbes-Robertson and his wife Gertrude Elliott, but it was first performed in

March 1899 by Mrs Patrick Campbell's company at the Theatre Royal, Newcastle.

Shaw was an outspoken critic of the establishment and unsurprisingly his play is more concerned with politics than love. Caesar is a far less romantic character than Antony and although Cleopatra is much younger in this version, she is never the silly girl and sidekick sister of Ptolemy, but a shrewd operator who plays the game of realpolitik very well. It was this play, rather than the better known Shakespeare version, that was translated to the screen via Hollywood.

On the eve of the First World War, Massenet wrote his opera *Cleopatre*. The man specialized in classical themes – he wrote one on Spartacus too – and Maria Kuznetsova, the darling of St Petersburg society under the last tsar, played the queen. There was a surreal echo here, had the Russians only known it. They were celebrating the end of the Ptolemies at the same time that revolutionaries had plans to topple the Romanovs.

But there is a sense in which Cleopatra is too big for the stage. Her ambitions, her contradictions, her sheer variety, dwarf the confines of theatre. As George Bernard Shaw said in 1945, 'What scope! What limitless possibilities! Here you have the whole world to play with!'

He was talking about the Denham Studios in London, but in reality he was talking about film.

18

GODDESS OF THE SILVER SCREEN

HOLLYWOODLAND, AD 1917

The celluloid Cleopatra was huge. Cecil B. DeMille's 1934 production poster showed the leads in a cinematic clinch and paraphrased Poe[78] with, 'The glory that was Egypt! The grandeur that was Rome!' It boasted 8,000 extras (long before CGI made all that humanity unnecessary), it took a year to make – then a *very* long haul in film production – and its lavish sets covered 400,000 square feet. Cleopatra's barge became 'a love boat' 500 feet long and her war-galleys were locked in a holocaust at sea while Antony's armies battled on land. This was the backdrop to a 'love affair that shook the world set in a spectacle of thrilling magnificence'.

But DeMille's was not the first film of the queen of Egypt. Georges Méliès produced the first known version as a 'short' in 1899, the same year that Shaw's play was performed.

Shortly after Beerbohm Tree played Antony on the stage in London and Maria Kuznetsova wowed them operatically in tsarist Russia, the Fox company launched Theda Bara down the Hollywood Nile in the silent version of 1917.

Early film-makers drew heavily on the Bible for their inspiration and in the days before the puritanical Hayes Commission began to introduce its rigid censorship, bacchanalian orgies and decadence were the stuff of ancient courts presided over by cruel tyrants. Theda Bara was a 'natural' for Cleopatra who fitted the licentious image perfectly. She was *the* vamp of the silent screen, a femme fatale with painted lips and large, hypnotic eyes. Her name, people said, was an apt anagram of 'Arab Death' and she hardly had to change her costume at all the following year for her role as Salome.

The sets of the 1917 film are astonishing, the painted columns of her chamber straight out of the Valley of the Kings while black American extras stand picturesquely as Nubian slaves fanning Cleopatra with ostrich feathers. She lounges casually on a chaise longue that Tutankhamun could have owned while an imperious-looking Caesar (Fritz Leiber) is attempting to control her by wearing plastic armour and a laurel wreath.

The 1934 version was more lavish and altogether on a different plane. Warren William played Caesar and heart-throb/hunk Henry Wilcoxon was Antony. The surprise came with Claudette Colbert as Cleopatra; she had previously only been known for her light comedy and romantic roles, but she was excellent as the Egyptian queen. In keeping with the world's distorted view of Cleopatra, DeMille asked Colbert whether she wanted to play one of the wickedest women in history. The action spans the involvement of both Caesar and Antony in Egypt and some film experts regard this *Cleopatra* as DeMille's best film. It was a 'talkie', of course, and filmed in black and white. Much of its set-piece brilliance owes a great deal to Busby Berkeley's mass dance routines in which dozens of luscious female slaves move as one to a huge backdrop of ostrich feathers.

The seduction scene of Antony by Cleopatra is superbly handled. Antony is furious at being kept waiting by the queen (nobody glowered quite like Henry Wilcoxon!) and she blasts him when she finally arrives with her choreographed slaves, lifting virgins in nets from the sea and scooping up handfuls of jewels.

'As Antony finally embraces her,' wrote Baird Searles, 'she looks across his shoulder, her face suddenly an icy mask and nods to her chamberlain. The camera pulls back from their feather-backed dais across the space of the hall. Gauzy drapes fall in front of the dais. Rose petals rain down. Dancing girls writhe…' and the scene unfolds to reveal Cleopatra's giant barge, which becomes the 'scene of an aphrodisiac rite timed to the rhythm of the oarsmen'. White peacocks abound, harpists play and there is even a virgin straddling a sacrificial ox swathed in garlands of flowers. The Apis bull had made it to the big screen.

The next venture was Shaw's *Caesar and Cleopatra*, released in 1946 and the one in which the playwright was closely involved. It was then the most expensive British film ever made, produced in an atmosphere of escapism from the austerity of post-war Britain. The lighthouse of Pharos, one of the world's seven wonders, was recreated and the cast was one to match DeMille's. Claude Rains played Caesar like a kind old uncle and the impossibly handsome Stewart Granger was Apollodorus, Cleopatra's faithful servant. So magnetic was Granger, said one critic, that it makes 'one wonder about Cleopatra's taste in men'. Flora Robson was the slave Ftatateeta and came dangerously close to stealing the film from Vivien Leigh. Even so, the star of *Gone with the Wind* put in a remarkable performance, maturing from impulsive girl to accomplished stateswoman.

All these versions were swept away by Joseph L. Mankiewicz's 1963 offering, made infamous by the on- and off-set romance between Elizabeth Taylor and Richard Burton and a colossal overspend that threatened at one point to bankrupt the Fox organization. The cost was $44 million (about $308 million in today's figures). Mankiewicz was a highly literate director and his screenplay acknowledged the services of men we have met before – Plutarch, Suetonius and Appian. Some critics believed that it was the attempt to stick to *history* as opposed to spectacle that caused *Cleopatra* to flop. Mankiewicz based the screenplay on *The Life and Times of Cleopatra* by Carlo Maria Franzero, which, while it followed the conventional (Romanized) facts, could not help seeing Cleopatra as a siren, 'deflowered, in the old custom', on the altar of Amun-Ra.[79] The film ran for nearly four hours and became, in a sense, the story of a domestic triangle – Caesar, Antony, Cleopatra – albeit on a colossal scale. The epics of the 1960s, no less than the SFX block-busters of today, received huge hype ahead of the premiere and, as today, it was usually woefully over the top.

The epic scenes, like Cleopatra's entry into Rome on a huge, slave-carried Sphinx, are dazzling in their glitter, but there is something predictable and laboured about them. Taylor's make-up was straight out of the wall-paintings at Luxor, but critics even complained about that, preferring the chic 1930s fashions of designer Travis Banton in the DeMille version. The battle of Actium was surprisingly well done in an age before computer graphics.

What of the actors? As George MacDonald Fraser says in his *Hollywood History of the World*, the arrival of the cult of celebrity adds to the problem of authenticity. 'They are not Antony and Caesar, they are Burton and Harrison.'[80] And even more so, they are Taylor. Rex Harrison is surely too urbane and 'modern' for one of the greatest generals in history and although we know that Burton could probably have held his own drink for drink with Antony, he is too petulant and too intelligent at least for Plutarch's thug. On the other hand, he handles the ennui after the Parthian campaign and after Actium very well. He *does* nothing and it is precisely that that infuriates us. We want to shake him and shout, 'You are Mark Antony, for God's sake! Pull yourself together!' Roddy McDowall is chillingly creepy as the single-minded Octavian, but could the real man who would become the Emperor Augustus have been *such* a psychopath? Elizabeth Taylor had more costume-changes than anyone in the cast, to accentuate Cleopatra's legendary wealth, but she was not merely a clotheshorse. She is endearing in the soft interchanges with both Caesar and Antony, imperious in command and genuinely, it seems, in love. She dies as nobly as Antony, proving that the Romans did not have a monopoly on courage.

The truth is that Cleopatra is a very difficult role to recreate, be it on stage or screen. Her sheer diversity defies belief and it all comes back to a question we have posed earlier – how could a woman cope against the male-dominated powers of the world, especially when that power was the greatest military machine in history?

As I write, a new *Cleopatra* is in the offing. Chat rooms have been abuzz since the summer of 2010 with Hollywood-generated gossip that Pulitzer Prize winner Stacy Shiff's

Cleopatra: A Life has been bought up by producer Scott Rudin with a view to present yet another celluloid version. Plans for a 3D rock 'n' roll musical based on Cleopatra by Steven Soderbergh appear to have died and in October, James '*LA Confidential*' Cameron was in discussions to direct. By November that was ruled out but controversy has arisen because of the potential casting of the queen. The likely choice is Angelina Jolie, whom Sony's production head Amy Pascal says was 'born to play this role'.

But there is a problem. *Essence* magazine wrote in June, 'Why does Hollywood think it's even slightly plausible to cast white women in roles that would be more sensible to cast a black actress for? Especially when that role is an African queen.' *Essence* has missed the point spectacularly. We shall discuss this more fully in the next chapter, but basically, Cleopatra was Greek. Being queen of Egypt does not remotely make her African in the accepted sense and the whole thing is a storm in a teacup. If we follow this thing logically, Spartacus would be played by a Bulgarian, Jesus by an Israeli and, of course, every Roman would be Italian. Caucasian American actors could not start to compete for roles before the sixteenth century!

Stacy Schiff herself has produced an element of sanity by giving an interview to the *Wall Street Journal* in November: 'If you need someone to project raw charisma and immense authority, I think [Angelina Jolie] is terrific. The interesting thing about Cleopatra is that she is such a shape-shifter ... throughout history we've moulded her to our times and our places.'

19

FATALE MONSTRUM?

'Moulded her to our times and our places.' This is the fate of any great figure from history. However much we try, through scholarship and careful research, we can never truly get under the skin of Cleopatra because she is not of our time. Intellectual as she was, she could not read the words you are reading now because in her day there was no such language. The last 2,000 years with all its experiences, especially for women, have changed irrevocably anything Cleopatra knew.

Yet there are some constants. The rampant xenophobia and sexism of the Romans has not disappeared, however much the Politically Correct brigade might wish it otherwise and it is still possible to accept the Roman propaganda view of Cleopatra as *fatale monstrum*, an unnatural and deadly harpy whose claws drew the blood of Julius Caesar and Mark Antony and the thousands of ordinary men who marched under her banner. As I write, the people of Alexandria are rioting in the streets, complaining about their government rather as their forebears snapped at the rule of the Ptolemies. Images on the television news of the mob clambering over the statue of Alexander the Great strikes a chord. The statue is relatively new, but the man and his age and his royal descendants take us back into the mists of time.

Cleopatra is rarely out of the news. She is the stock-in-trade of television documentary-makers, either in her own right or as part of a programme/series on Rome. High-profile archaeology has thrown its spotlight on her too. Serious underwater research has been going on since 1994 in the harbour of Alexandria, which Octavian's Romans called Portus Magnus, the great port. A series of earthquakes since Cleopatra's time, which may or may not have been accompanied by at least one tsunami in AD 365, have drowned the palaces of the Ptolemies. Land erosion and the rising of sea levels have added to the problem. Over the last fifteen years two parallel underwater projects have been going on led by Dr Zahi Hawass, secretary general of the supreme council of antiquities of Egypt, and Franck Goddio, a specialist undersea archaeologist. Their finds are extraordinary – huge blocks of sculpted stone that may have come from the Pharos lighthouse, life-size statues of pharaohs and gods, in Greek and Egyptian style, from the royal palaces, sheets of gold with Greek texts written on them. Isis and Osiris have been found lying in the silt, along with the bearded Serapis.

In May 2008, Zahi Hawass announced that he had found Cleopatra's tomb. Land-based archaeology is being carried out in Alexandria and at Heraclion and Canopus along the coast, but Hawass' Cleopatra site is at Taposiris Magna, 28 miles west of the queen's capital. The underground chambers there have yielded many Cleopatra coins and busts which have her likeness. One 400-foot-long tunnel also has coins of Mark Antony. The only problem is that no bodies have come to light and without them the whole claim can be no more than conjecture. John Baines, Professor of Egyptology at Oxford University, warned that looking for royal tombs is a hopeless task and doubted very much that Octavian would have allowed the queen to be buried with Antony.[81]

The problem arises because we do not know exactly where the pair were buried or indeed if they were buried together. Cassius Dio says they were and from his texts and those of Plutarch it is clear that Cleopatra's mausoleum, where she died, was in the palace area, presumably in Alexandria's Beta district. We know that Octavian allowed their burial with full funeral rites, but this does not give us a site. Taposiris Magna is a full day's ride (and two days on foot) from those palaces and the place, unlike Alexandria, has no particular resonance as a burial site of the Ptolemies.

Adrian Goldsworthy wrote in his recent book that he secretly hoped the tombs would never be found. 'Neither Cleopatra nor Antony enjoyed much peace in their lives,' he says, and 'it would seem a shame if their remains ended up on display to crowds of tourists, or even examined, stored and catalogued in a museum basement.'[82] Three lines earlier, however, the historian in him admits that any new discoveries would be of interest.

Enter another piece of speculation hyped by the media into spectacular fact. Two years ago, the BBC produced a documentary with the lurid (and woefully incorrect) title *Cleopatra: Portrait of a Killer* and it focused on the archaeology of a tomb in Ephesus that was claimed to be that of Arsinoe, Cleopatra's younger sister. The find itself was old hat (the tomb having been opened by archaeologists in 1926) but state-of-the-art research was only carried out in the three years prior to the programme. The Ephesus body was found in an octagonal-shaped tomb, which was very unusual, and the skeleton lay in a sarcophagus. The skull was measured and examined, but ended up in Nazi Germany during the Second World War and subsequently disappeared. In the early 1990s, Hike Thür of the Austrian Academy of Sciences re-entered the tomb and carried out extensive work on the remaining bones. Fabian Kranz worked on the body from 2007 and came to the following conclusions. The carbon dating process gave a date range of 200–220 BC, which fits Arsinoe, and the woman in question would have been between the ages of fifteen and eighteen. There was no sign of disease or that the girl had ever done hard manual work. That this *could* be the body of Arsinoe cannot be doubted, but there are more cons than pros in the evidence.

First, it was asserted that the octagonal tomb shape bears reference to the Pharos lighthouse with which Arsinoe was associated. The octagon was, in fact, the shape of only one tier of the lighthouse – the others were rectangular and circular – and there is no written reference linking Arsinoe with the Pharos at all. Secondly, all accounts agree that she was executed in or near the temple of Artemis, probably by Antony's guards. We obviously do not know how this was done, but it seems unlikely that soldiers/hitmen would waste time with poison when they were carrying swords. There is no sign of violent trauma on the Ephesus body; sword thrusts or hacks could leave telltale cuts on the bones – there were none. Ages are notoriously difficult in body

identification and we do not have any exact date of birth for
Arsinoe, but all written records imply that she was four or
five years younger than Cleopatra. That means that at the
time of her death in 41, Arsinoe was twenty-three or twenty-
four, not the teenager the skeletal remains suggest. Then
there is the vexed question of the state of the body. Ephesus
had been under Greek control for 200 years by 41 and the
Greeks practised cremation of their dead. The Ptolemaic
Egyptians, as we know, practised mummification. Why,
then, has the body of Arsinoe undergone neither of these
processes?

The most contentious theory, however, comes with the
skull. It has gone, so we are relying on measurements taken
in the 1920s, a time when archaeology was notoriously
lacking in intellectual rigour, and the conclusion reached in
the 2009 programme was that the skull was peculiarly elongated, which was an African practice. This means that
Arsinoe was of mixed race. We know that her father was
Ptolemy Auletes, a Greek, so her mother had to be African.
Because she was Cleopatra's sister, the theory runs,
Cleopatra was black too. It is difficult to know where to
start to unravel these leaps in logic. Elongated skulls are
found in many cultures, including that of the Huns of
Eastern Europe, the Slavs and Russians, the Incas and in
Greece itself. Allowing that this is not a peculiarity of this
particular body – perhaps hydrocephaly which distorts the
skull was responsible – but a genetic trait, then it could well
mean that 'Arsinoe's' mother as well as her father was
Greek. Then we have the further leap that Arsinoe and
Cleopatra had the same mother. We do not know that. It is
entirely possible that all Auletes' children were by different
women. All we can say is that the Ephesus body is that of a

high-status young female, cause of death unknown, who was buried in the Octagon in the 200 years before the birth of Christ. Infuriatingly, it is as vague as that.

In 2009 Egyptologist Dr Sally Ashton of Cambridge University compiled a computerized face of Cleopatra to help us understand what Chaucer's 'rose' and Shakespeare's 'ribaudred nag' actually looked like. The result is typical of all computer-generated images – it could be anybody. Factored into the computer program for this was every known image of Cleopatra, including Greek busts, Alexandrian coins and Egyptian bas-reliefs. Most contentious of all is the skin pigmentation. None of the artefacts mentioned can help us with that and no contemporary comments on it. Deep down, we *want* Cleopatra to be dark-skinned and sultry, because it fits with all our prejudices and preconceptions. An auburn-haired, poppy-eyed Greek woman with a hooked nose and hard mouth does not equate with the siren who challenged an empire and destroyed her own.

It has taken a long time for the world to escape the cultural shackles of the Roman historians. Shakespeare didn't even try. Not until 1838 was there a book about Cleopatra written by a woman. *Memoirs of Celebrated Female Sovereigns* was written in that year by Anna Brownell Jameson. The purpose of the book was to 'present in a small compass ... an idea of the influence which a female government has had generally on men and nations and of the influence which the possession of power has had individually on the female character',[83] but the author admits that she sometimes breaks the rules of biography by going for the moral or picturesque. In the case of morality, of course, she was doing no more than Plutarch in his *Parallel*

Lives but the moral high ground had changed somewhat in 1,800 years. For example, she finds it absurd that victories are always called 'glorious' and is appalled that the sheer brutality of history is far more horrific than 'any of the banished superstitions and goblins of the nursery'.

Mrs Jameson was fully aware of the 1830s' limitations of female power and even rights. As she was writing, the eighteen-year-old Victoria was struggling through the first year of her reign. She was arguably the most powerful woman in the world and the same age as Cleopatra when she assumed that position in 48 BC. But Victoria was surrounded by male advisers, a male Privy Council, a male parliament and those few allowed to vote for her political parties were all men. So natural is this order of things, says Mrs Jameson, that when a bizarre collection of circumstances leads to female rule, the female in question is always *in extremis* just trying to cope. She cites Christina of Sweden, 'the acute Elizabeth' [the First, of England], the 'haughty energetic Catherine' [the Great, of Russia], the 'stupid, heartless Anne' [of England] and the 'amiable' [Austrian Empress] Maria Theresa. She concludes, rather sadly, that the rules of these queens and others she includes in this book have been either 'conspicuously unhappy or criminal' and that female government is not 'properly or naturally that of the sceptre or the sword'. Did she really believe this? Why not – she was a woman of her times. Victoria may have been the most powerful woman in the world, but she deferred constantly to her male supporters – her uncle Leopold of the Belgians, her husband Prince Albert, her Prime Minister Benjamin Disraeli. It was the way of things.

And so Mrs Jameson is scathing of Cleopatra – 'as a woman, she can scarcely be said to claim either our sympathy or our respect; as a sovereign, she neither achieved great exploits nor great conquests'. But she has to agree that Cleopatra left behind a name that 'still acts as a spell upon the fancy'. While acknowledging the classical authors' writings on Cleopatra's lovely voice and philosophical learning, Mrs Jameson adds that she was 'dissembling, ambitious, vain, perverse and utterly unprincipled'. This was 1838 and Mrs Jameson has to be coy about the Cleopatra/Caesar relationship. No sacrifice was too great for Cleopatra, however, including 'her sex's honour', and later her enemies 'could easily guess at the means by which Cleopatra had seduced her judge'.

She does not believe that Cleopatra had her own brother Ptolemy XIV murdered to clear the way for Caesarion. There is no direct evidence for it and it 'bespeaks a heart more completely hardened against the natural affections than Cleopatra ever exhibited'. She was not warlike but ruled by 'policy and prudence'.

Mrs Jameson is dismissive of Antony, too. He was the 'arbitrator of her fate and he ended by becoming the veriest slave that was ever chained to a woman's footstool'. He was 'a magnificent, reckless libertine, a valiant but a coarse soldier'. True to form, Cleopatra is the villainess of Actium, losing her nerve and hoisting her sails with the feckless Antony, made mad by the gods out to destroy him, following suit. The author does concede, however, that the queen easily duped Octavian – 'she had seen through his mean designs and his deep disguises'.

Anna Jameson follows Plutarch with a grim determination perhaps to prove that women were just as good historians as men. She was writing at the end of the antiquarian period when any kind of folk tale was believed and before history became critical and a matter of interpretation. Her conclusion, however, is interesting because it transcends all that – 'thus perished this celebrated woman [she goes with the asp poisoning] whose character exhibits such an extraordinary mixture of grandeur and littleness and whose life and fate present something so wildly magnificent to the fancy, that we dare not try her by the usual rules of conduct'. We must leave her as we find her – 'a dazzling piece of witchcraft'.

Not until 1914 was there a balanced thesis that put her into the context of Egyptian history. It was *The Life and Times of Cleopatra, Queen of Egypt*, written by the archaeologist Arthur Weigall. This is a real attempt for the first time to see her as she really was – 'an often lonely and sorely tried woman, who fought all her life for the fulfilment of a patriotic and splendid ambition ...'[84]

Look on the Internet today and you will find over 18,000,000 sites devoted to Cleopatra. You can buy make-up, wigs, necklaces and even lingerie. You can play slot games and read about various exhibitions you'll kick yourself for having missed. Nobody has tried, as far as I am aware, to turn Cleopatra into a feminist icon – her story is too wound up with men for that. Only a few scholars share the view of the Arab traveller Al-Masudi from the seventh century – 'She was a sage, a philosopher, who elevated the ranks of scholars and enjoyed their company.'[85] Most people believe she was Egyptian and many are still ready to accept the Roman libel, brilliantly summed up by historian Joyce Tyldesley – 'Cleopatra ... was to be remembered as that immoral foreign woman. Almost overnight she became the most frightening of Roman stereotypes; an unnatural woman. A woman who worshipped crude gods, dominated men, slept with her brothers and gave birth to bastards. A woman foolish enough to think she might one day rule Rome and devious enough to lure a decent man [Caesar or Antony, Octavian or Herod, take your pick] away from his hearth and home.'[86]

Stacy Schiff summarizes superbly too – 'Many people have spoken for her, including the greatest playwrights and poets; we have been putting words in her mouth for two thousand years. In one of the busiest afterlives in history, she has gone on to become an asteroid, a video game, a cliché, a cigarette, a slot machine, a strip club, a synonym for Elizabeth Taylor. Shakespeare attested to Cleopatra's infinite variety. He had no idea.'[87]

And in the end, in a way, Cleopatra has won. She has survived the scurrilous attacks on her, which called her harlot, witch, sorceress, *fatale monstrum*. But she has survived the probing intrusions of the good guys, too, those of us, historians, archaeologists and the rest, who have tried to find the truth about her. 'So far,' says the website of the recent Cleopatra Exhibition at the Franklin Institute, Philadelphia, 'the real last queen of Egypt has eluded everyone.'

NOTES

1 The top section collapsed in AD 796 and subsequent earthquakes over the centuries flattened it. The fifteenth-century fortress of Sultan Quait Bey stands on the site today.

2 The name means seven stades (1 stade = 600 feet).

3 Philo *Embassy to Gaius* 149–51 trans. F. H. Coulson, quoted in Tyldesley p 93.

4 It must have been rather like the gigantic palace of the dictator Nicolai Ceausescu in Bucharest. Only the centre of this vast building is still used as government offices; the rest is one huge, echoing mausoleum to a failed regime.

5 Strabo quoted in Barry Cunliffe *Rome and Her Empire* p 232.

6 Suchos was the Greek name for Sobek, the crocodile-god.

7 Strabo quoted in Barry Cunliffe *Rome and Her Empire* p 233.

8 Strabo quoted in Barry Cunliffe *Rome and Her Empire* p 233.

9 These terms are arbitrary and designed to help with understanding. They do not conform exactly to what is a notoriously controversial classification in the modern world.

10 Guy de la Bédoyère *Gods with Thunderbolts; Religion in Roman Britain* (Stroud: Tempus, 2002) p 16.

11 Plato quoted in Fletcher p 29.

12 Although Alexander's detractors point out that his astonishing campaign's success against the Persians was achieved by only three battles – Granicus (334), Issus (333) and Gaugamala (331).

13 Arrian (AD 86–160) *History of Events After Alexander* quoted in Fletcher p 38.

14 In the twentieth century, the embalmed body of Vladimir Ilich Ulyanov (Lenin) held a similarly sacred place in the hearts of his followers with queues filing past it in Moscow's Red Square every day.

15 Although her daughter called herself Cleopatra Selene (the moon) she did not rule Egypt as her mother had done.

16 Herodotus II 46, quoted in Fletcher p 49.

17 All this is highly dubious. Today's African elephants are larger, not smaller than their Indian counterparts and are notoriously difficult to train, so accounts of their role at Raphia must be taken with more than a pinch of salt.

18 Quoted in Fletcher p 55.

19 The instrument was more like an oboe than a flute, but
    both versions are used in Auletes' context.

20 The information in this section comes from *Motherhood
    and Childbirth in Pharaonic Egypt* S. Ashoush and A.
    Fahmy, Lectures in the Department of Obstetrics and
    Gynaecology, Ain Shams University.

21 Quoted in Fletcher p 57.

22 Livy *History of Rome* 1.31

23 Plutarch *Lives – Numa XVII*, quoted in Anthony
    Kamm *The Romans* (London: Routledge, 1995) p 9.

24 Livy *History of Rome* 1.49.

25 Cicero *The Laws* III.3 quoted in Kamm p 10.

26 Livy *History of Rome* X5.

27 Vegetus, quoted in Hughes and Forrest *The Romans
    Discover Britain* (CUP, 1981) p 35.

28 This is not an original term; it means segmented breast-
    plate but we have no idea what the Romans called it.

29 Quoted in Philip Matyszak *The Chronicle of the Roman
    Republic* p 165.

30 The father of Shakespeare's Enobarbus.

31 The Oscan language is an early form of Latin.

32 Quoted in Matyszak *Chronicle of the Roman Republic*
    p 201.

33 Ibid.

34 Legions' marching song, Suetonius *Life of Caesar,* quoted
    in Matyszak p 200.

35 See Tom Holland, *Rubicon.*

36 Cicero – *Second Oration Against Catiline* quoted in
    Matyszak p 213.

37 Quoted in Fletcher *Cleopatra the Great* p 80.

38 Funerary stela quoted in Tyldesley p 42.

39 Plutarch, *Life of Caesar* ch 15.

40 Petronius, *Who's Who in the Roman World* (London: Routledge, 2001).

41 Holland, *Rubicon* p 309.

42 The name given to the hob-nailed sandal worn by soldiers.

43 Quoted in Matyszak p 207.

44 Plutarch *Pompey* trans Rex Warner p 241.

45 Ibid.

46 This is indeed how it was done in *Carry On Cleo* (1964) with Amanda Barrie as the queen and Kenneth Williams as Caesar.

47 Stacy Schiff *Cleopatra, A Life* (Virgin, 2010) p 241 taken from Lucan.

48 The Roman term for the Mediterranean was *mare nostrum,* our sea.

49 By the English explorers Speke, Burton and Baker in the 1860s and 1870s.

50 This is evidenced from a stela now in the Louvre, Paris, and is not necessarily accurate as it refers to 'king Caesar', a title given to Caesarion nowhere else.

51 Most commentators today translate this as a telegram – 'came; saw; conquered'. For those of us old enough to have 'done' Latin at school, this is nonsense. The 'I' is understood in this part of speech.

52 There were several of these in late republican Rome. The colosseum had yet to be built.

53 Re-enactments like this were still taking place in circuses into the twentieth century. In Britain the Royal Tournament at London's Earl's Court is a survivor of this sort of entertainment.

54 Cicero *Letters to Atticus* 15:15.2 trans L. P. Wilkinson 1972.

55 As described by Suetonius, Appian and Plutarch, but it may be pure legend.

56 There is a long tradition of royal survival in history, with Arthur sleeping under his hill until his country needs him and the tsarevitch Alexei surviving the hail of bullets in the House of Special Purpose at Ekaterinburg in 1918.

57 Erik Durschmied *The Hinge Factor: How Chance and Stupidity Have Changed History* (London Coronet, 1999).

58 See Chapter 15.

59 Cicero, quoted in Schiff p 151.

60 Quoted in Schiff p 150.

61 The lack of stirrups in the ancient world made cavalry less impressive than it became later with them. A recent television mini-series used stirrups on the grounds of health and safety!

62 I believe the same is true of Vespasian who took Vectis, the Isle of Wight, in AD 43. There is no evidence of any opposition from the islanders.

63 Cicero *Ad Atticus* 7, 8.

64 Except perhaps 'genistho'.

65 Cicero *Ad Atticus* 10, 10.

66 For all his Greekness, Plutarch was essentially as Roman a writer as Josephus, the Jewish chronicler who 'came over to Rome' in the first century AD.

67 Goldsworthy *Antony and Cleopatra* p 273.

68 Which is why, partly, Rome was so horrified by Boudicca in AD 60. The woman actually led her warriors in person.

69 Suetonius *Augustus* 69.

70 In the 1963 film, Roddy McDowell's Octavian went one better and hurled the spear into the heart of Cleopatra's ambassador.

71 Quoted in Schiff p 243.

72 Cassius Dio *The Reign of Augustus* trans Ian Scott-Kilvert, Penguin p 59.

73 Cassius Dio *The Reign of Augustus* trans Ian Scott-Kilvert, Penguin p 61.

74 Horace *Odes* Book I No 37 1914 trans. Quoted in *History of Quotations*, Cohen and Major.

75 Cassius Dio *Histories* 51:15 trans E. Cary.

76 Josephus *Against Apion*.

77 Selgado. No source.

78 To Helen 1845

79 Carlo Maria Franzero *The Life and Times of Cleopatra* quoted in Joyce Tyldesley p 216.

80 Fraser *Hollywood History of the World* p 18.

81 There are huge gaps in the royal tomb record. The vast majority of the Ptolemies were buried in Alexandria, yet none of their bodies has been conclusively found. Likewise, we have no clear idea what became of the body of Alexander the Great after its removal from the Soma.

82 Goldsworthy, *Antony and Cleopatra* (London: Weidenfeld and Nicolson, 2010) p 395.

83 All quotations from Jameson *Memoirs of Celebrated Female Sovereigns* 1838 pp 31–57.

84 Arthur Weigall 1924 ed vi.

85 Al-Masudi, quoted in Tyldesley p 212.

86 Joyce Tyldesley, p 206.

87 Stacy Schiff *Cleopatra, A Life* p 1.

SELECT BIBLIOGRAPHY

Appian, trans Carter, John, *The Civil Wars* (London: Penguin, 1996).

Bradford, Ernle, *Cleopatra* (London: Hodder and Stoughton, 1972).

Campbell, Duncan, *Greek and Roman Artillery* (Oxford: Osprey, 2003).

de la Bèdoyére, Guy, *Gods with Thunderbolts* (Stroud: Tempus, 2002).

Dio, Cassius, trans Scott-Kilvert, Ian, *The Roman History: The Reign of Augustus* (London: Penguin, 1987).

Fletcher, Joann, *Cleopatra the Great* (London: Hodder and Stoughton, 2008).

Fraser, George MacDonald, *The Hollywood History of the World* (London: Michael Joseph, 1988).

Goldsworthy, Adrian, *The Complete Roman Army* (London: Thames and Hudson, 2003).

— —, *Antony and Cleopatra* (London: Weidenfeld and Nicolson, 2010).

— —, *Roman Warfare* (London: Cassell & Co, 2002).

Goodman, Martin, *The Roman World* (London: Routledge, 1997).

Grant, Michael, *From Alexander to Cleopatra: the Hellenistic World* (London: Weidenfeld and Nicholson, 1982).

Hazel, John, *Who's Who in the Roman World* (London: Routledge, 2001).

Holland, Tom, *Rubicon* (London: Abacus, 2004).

Hutchinson, *Dictionary of Ancient and Medieval Warfare* (Oxford: Helicon, 1998).

Jameson, Mrs, *Memoirs of Celebrated Female Sovereigns* (New York: Harper Bros, 1838).

Kamm, Anthony, *The Romans* (London: Routledge, 1995).

Lewis, Naphtali and Reinhold, Meyer, *Roman Civilization Vol I: The Republic and the Augustan Age* (New York: Columbia UP, 1990).

Matyszak, Philip, *The Enemies of Rome* (London: Thames and Hudson, 2004).

— —, *Chronicle of the Roman Republic* (London: Thames and Hudson, 2003).

Peddie, John, *The Roman War Machine* (Stroud: Sutton, 2004).

Plutarch, trans Warner, Rex, *Fall of the Roman Republic* (London: Penguin, 1972).

Pomeroy, Sarah, *Goddesses, Whores, Wives and Slaves* (London: Pimlico, 1994).

Salgado, Gamini, *The Elizabethan Underworld* (London: BCA, 1977).

Santosuosso, Antonio, *Storming the Heavens* (London: Pimlico, 2004).

Scarre, Chris, *Historical Atlas of Ancient Rome* (London: Penguin, 1995).

Schiff, Stacy, *Cleopatra, A Life* (London: Virgin Books, 2010).

Searles, Baird, *Epic! History on the Big Screen* (New York: Harry Abrams Inc, 1990).

Sckunda, Nicholas et al, *Caesar's Legions* (Oxford: Osprey, 2000).

Shakespeare, William, *Antony and Cleopatra.*

Shaw, George Bernard, *Caesar and Cleopatra.*

Sifakis, Carl, *Encyclopaedia of Assassinations* (New York: Headline, 1993).

Southern, Pat, *Pompey the Great* (Stroud: Tempus, 2002).

Trow, M. J., *Spartacus, the Myth and the Man* (Stroud: Sutton, 2006).

Tyldesley, Joyce, *Cleopatra, Last Queen of Egypt* (London: Profile Books, 2009).

Volkmann, Hans, *Cleopatra: A Study in Politics and Propaganda* 1959.

von Wertheimer, Oskar, *Cleopatra, A Regal Voluptuary* 1931.

Weigall, Arthur, *The Life and Times of Cleopatra, Queen of Egypt* (London: William Blackwood and Sons, 1914).

Williams, Derek, *Romans and Barbarians* (New York: St Martin's Press, 1999).

INDEX